STAN LAUREL AND OTHER
STARS OF THE PANOPTICON

THE STORY OF THE BRITANNIA MUSIC HALL

STAN LAUREL
AND OTHER STARS OF THE
PANOPTICON

THE STORY OF THE BRITANNIA MUSIC HALL

JUDITH BOWERS

BIRLINN

First published in 2007 by
Birlinn Limited
West Newington House
10 Newington Road
Edinburgh
EH9 1QS

www.birlinn.co.uk

ISBN10: 1 84158 617 X
ISBN13: 978 1 84158 617 5

British Library Cataloguing-in-Publication Data
A catalogue record for this book is available
from the British Library.

Design and typeset by Melvin Creative
Printed and bound by The Cromwell Press, Trowbridge, Wiltshire

*To the memories of the performers, staff and patrons who once
populated the Britannia Panopticon Music Hall*

CONTENTS

ACKNOWLEDGEMENTS

The author wishes to thank the following for their help with the book and their participation in the Britannia Panopticon project over the years:

The Mitchell Family, Graham Hunter, Fin Mclay, Euan Adamson, Peter Longman, Anthony Duda, Paul Maloney, Minty Donald, Peter Longman, David Walker, The Mitchell Library, the University of Glasgow Special Collection, People's Palace Museum, Dr Vanessa Toulmin and the National Fairground Archive at the University of Sheffield, the Theatres Trust of Great Britain, Betty and Hugh McLaughlin, Fay Lenore, Voltini, James Kelly, Harry Hill, Tony Perry, The Sons of the Desert, A.J. Marriot, Mike Fraser, the Glasgow Building Preservation Trust, the Merchant City Townscape Heritage Initiative, Liz Davidson, Euan Curtis, the Britannia Panopticon Music Hall Trust and the Friends of the Britannia Panopticon Music Hall Trust, Helen Campbell, Magda Shukis, the volunteers, the Mitchell girls and the many folk who have told me their stories on open days in the Britannia Panopticon Music Hall.

PROLOGUE

As a young girl, one of my favourite books was C.S. Lewis's *The Lion, the Witch and the Wardrobe*. I was mesmerised by the idea of opening an ordinary wardrobe door, pushing past a few old coats and finding a completely different and wonderful world on the other side – a world filled with magic!

I spent a lot of my childhood poking around in wardrobes and opening all sorts of doors in pursuit of my own Narnia, but I never found it. Many years later, however, when I was 28, I discovered a very special door indeed. To my excitement, a magical, forgotten world lay just beyond it: the Britannia Panopticon.

1 TREASURES OF THE TRONGATE

Occasionally unsuspecting tourists stumble, bewildered, onto the Trongate, mistaking it for a continuation of the cosmopolitan Argyle Street. They stand looking around them with utter bemusement as the tidy stretch of smart precinct and fashionable chain stores seems to dissolve into a thoroughfare of pound shops and decaying architecture. They struggle to take in the sudden change of ambience. Then they find themselves confronted by one of the local characters, fresh from a morning of heavy drinking: ''Scuse me, have y' got ten pence for a cup o' tea?'

The Trongate is where you will find hard-working, salt-of-the-earth Glaswegians. Artists, musicians, young mums pushing prams, students, bargain hunters, *Big Issue* sellers and beggars swarm past the discount clothing stores, pawn shops, amusements arcades, furniture and DIY emporiums. Despite its reputation as the poor end of town, however, the Trongate was once the wealthiest area of Glasgow; amongst the cheap shop-fronts and general scruffiness, a wealth of fine architecture can still be found.

I first encountered the Trongate in 1990 when I began renting a unit just off Argyle Street, in the Virginia Galleries, a wonderful old tobacco auction house which still retained some of its original features. The auctioneer's box was still positioned above the main entrance doors, although it had been converted into a public convenience; shops which had once sold sugar, coffee, tea and other commodities lined the two tiers of galleries supported by slender cast-iron columns. There was a central courtyard and a glazed roof flooded the whole space with light on sunny days, leaving it dark and brooding on dull ones. The building had once been used as a location in the TV drama *The Duchess of Duke Street*, but when I was working there it was a little indoor bazaar that sold all sorts of books, collectables, antiques, clothes, candles, crystals and bric-a-brac, with the obligatory fortune teller located on the second floor.

Although the clean and busy Argyle Street was right on my office

Façade of the Britannia Music Hall

doorstep, I found the scruffier and cheaper Trongate, a few metres to the east, a far more interesting prospect for occasional lunchtime saunters. It was the street that the recent gentrification of Glasgow forgot, with an abundance of buildings diverse in architectural style and merit, from the seventeenth-century Tolbooth (the old city prison) to the more dubious architecture left behind by the modernist rebellion of the 1960s. It seemed tired and run-down, but still charming and intriguing in its decay. One building in particular had caught my eye.

I can remember looking at it for the first time from across the street. My attention was drawn by its colour, pale blue. It stood out like a sore thumb amidst its unpainted neighbours. The paint had begun to flake off in bits, revealing-buff coloured sandstone beneath and buddleia bushes were pushing their way out through the upper windows and guttering. The paint and neglect did not detract from the fact that this was a remarkable piece of architecture. 'Italianate' in style, the building had three floors of arched windows. Beautifully carved swags of fruit and Grecian key decoration adorned the façade, which rose in fading majesty above the uninspiring modern shop unit at street level. The building reminded me of an old Victorian lady in her crinoline, past her prime, but still standing stoic and sublime. It seemed quite incompatible with the tall, 1960s block of concrete just to the west.

The windows from the first floor up were empty, dark and lifeless. Like many buildings in the East End of the city, only the ground floor was occupied and the upper storeys were either used for storage or lay vacant. The windows on the first floor had been painted white and emblazoned with the words 'Leather Club'. There were leather jackets, coats and trousers in the window display of the shop below. I went in.

The ground floor gave no indication of the secrets I hoped lay hidden somewhere in this Victorian relic. Brightly lit, the shop was a forest of clothing rails and shelves which sagged beneath the weight of leather coats, skirts, trousers, jackets, dresses, belts, handbags, wallets, boots and shoes. Pushing through the leather forest, I found my way to a staircase which led up to the men's department on the first floor. At first, it seemed to be a repeat of the floor below and my heart sank, but only for a moment; my eyes were soon drawn to the ceiling. Although not instantly remarkable (there was no cornicing or ceiling rose), it bizarrely sloped up a few feet at either side of the expansive room. What was the reason for this strange arrangement? It certainly didn't appear to have been an intentional design feature – nothing of this shop's interior, in fact, appeared to be by design. I wandered amongst the clothes and garish promotional posters, scanning the room looking for any evidence of its Victorian origins. Hidden amongst the racks of imported leather jackets were big, cast-iron columns which appeared mismatched: on one side of the room, they were capped with ornate moulded detailing, partially filled in with thick black gloss paint, whilst on the other side they were plain. The columns were placed around the edges of the lowered ceiling and it reminded me of the slender poles that supported the tiers in the Virginia Galleries. It now seemed obvious that the ceiling was not original. I asked one of the shop assistants if she knew what the building had been used for previously. She looked at me with a glazed expression and replied in a thoroughly bored tone, 'A shop.'

I left a note for the manager, asking whether it would be possible for me to see the upper floors of the building, and then went back to work.

The shop manager never did get in touch and I gradually forgot about the building. It wasn't until 1993 that I once again found myself standing outside it, wondering what secrets lay hidden there. In fact, I had nipped into the lane at the east side of the building to light a cigarette. As I stood struggling with my match against the wind, I looked up and saw on the wall a plaque with a picture of the blue building on it. The drawing showed the façade, but half had been removed to reveal a theatre on the first and second floors. It was a bit like peeking into a dolls' house. Above the picture was written 'Britannia Music Hall 1857–1938' and beneath was a brief history of the building. From this plaque I learned that Stan Laurel had made his debut here and that a man called A.E. Pickard had changed the name of the building to 'Panopticon' when he had taken over as manager in 1906.

This was obviously a building of historical as well as architectural interest. The first-floor men's department of the Leather Club had once been the stalls of Britannia Music Hall. That explained the lowered ceiling on the first floor: the balcony must have been above. The question was, did any of it still survive? Ornate ceiling plaster, for example? Seating? Old back cloths and bits of scenery? A couple of years previously I had been in an old cinema which had been converted into a bingo hall. Above a lowered ceiling, the original plaster work was still there. Perhaps it had also survived here.

I stubbed out my cigarette and went into the shop to ask if there was any way that I might get a look at the floors above. I received a point-blank refusal and was told that the top floors were only used for storage and that there was nothing worth seeing.

Later that day I went to meet a friend. I had spent several months writing and researching for a murder tour: my friend, Steven (then a student at the Royal Scottish Academy of Music and Drama), was going to assist me in taking tourists round 'Glasgow's Victorian Square Mile of Murder', visiting some of the most famous murder sights of the city.

I told him about the powder-blue building and the plaque and that I was desperate to find out more. Steven then told me his lecturer had been in the building and that some seating and a projection room still survived. My interest was now well and truly piqued and I decided I needed to find out more about it.

Over the next few years I trawled through books and old newspapers, trying to find out as much as I could about the Britannia Music Hall. It was difficult to find any real information as, sadly, not many original documents pertaining to it as a working music hall survived. But through newspaper articles and adverts contemporary with the building as a music hall, I did manage to gather enough information to make it perfectly obvious to me that this was no ordinary theatre; this was a very early music hall with a list of performers that read like a directory of music-hall stars. Surely if any part of the auditorium survived, it should be investigated and recorded?

Occasionally I would try to gain access to the upper floors of the building, but without success. I would go up to the first floor and sneak around trying to pull up the edges of wallpaper and carpet to see what was beneath. I was always discovered before I could really see what was there. On a couple of occasions I tried to sneak out of the door marked 'Staff Only': beyond it was a sloped floor leading down to another door which I could never quite get to before being caught. I left a couple of notes, this time for the attention of the owner, but again, they were never replied to. Eventually the Leather Club closed and the ground floor was turned into an amusement arcade.

2 OPENING THE DOOR

One drizzly day near the end of February 1997, I was walking down the Trongate on my way back to my office, which was by this time in the old Candleriggs Market in the Merchant City. I was returning from a meeting and was feeling as miserable as the weather. As I wandered past the pale blue building and looked up, as was my habit, to the upper floors, I heard a tapping sound. On the other side of the shop window was Helen, an old friend from the Virginia Galleries. We hadn't seen each other for a couple of years, so I went into the arcade. Helen took me into a small staff area at the back of the amusements. As we sat drinking coffee, I began to quiz her about the building.

'Have you been upstairs?' I asked.

'I use the attic to store props in. I don't like it. I'm sure it's haunted. All sorts of weird things happen up there. Stuff moves about and I've heard strange noises. It's creepy.'

'Do you think you could take me upstairs?' I asked, at which point a door at the back of the staff area opened and in walked a man who joined us at the table and started chatting to us. Helen introduced him to me as the building's owner. At last, my chance had come. He seemed pleasant and friendly, so I began to ask him about the building. How much did he know about it? How much of the auditorium was left?

'There's not really very much left,' he replied. 'It's been sealed off for years and there really isn't anything to see. It's dark and I don't take people up there in case they fall through a floor.'

The glimmer of hope that I might one day be privy to the secrets that this building held began to fade. Although I had read that much of the auditorium was still extant, these articles were about ten years old and a lot could have happened since then. I had to see just what was left. I began telling the owner some of the history I had so far discovered. I told him about the debut of Stan Laurel in the building and how it was one of the last surviving early music halls in Britain. He listened patiently.

I pleaded with him to let me see the upper floors. 'I know you said that there isn't much left, but I worked on archaeological excavations for about four years and the experience has taught me a lot about looking for the clues left by the past. I only want a quick look, just to see what does survive, and if possible, at some point to come back and take a couple of photographs of anything that does remain, even if it is just a scrap of old plasterwork.' I desperately fluttered my eyelashes and Helen backed my plea, telling him that I was interested in Glasgow history and that I ran ghost tours. At length, he finally agreed to take me upstairs.

He went off to find the keys and I waited with Helen for his return. Excitement began to drum its fingers on the base of my spine; for years I had tried to get above the shop floors of this old building and now I had an opportunity to do so. I knew I might be disappointed when I got there, but there was also the chance that there was more evidence surviving than the owner let on.

He returned a few minutes later with a set of keys and a torch, and then he took me across the arcade to another door at the back of the bingo area. We went through this door and began to climb a brightly lit staircase which led to a half-landing, where there was another door. The owner unlocked it and suddenly I found myself stepping back into the past. As the door closed behind us the noise of the gaming machines and the bingo caller faded. The smell of freshly brewed coffee and cigarettes which had pervaded the amusements below was replaced by the smell of ancient wood and plaster. It felt as if time had suddenly stopped. My stiletto heels clicked on the stone steps as we made our way up the age-worn staircase, which spiralled up like those found in old Glasgow tenement closes. I put my hand on the heavy wooden banister and my fingers pushed away the thick layer of dust. The wood beneath had been worn smooth by the thousands of hands that must have grasped it as I did now. We stopped at another half-landing and another door. Suddenly I had butterflies in my stomach and for a moment I am sure I forgot to breathe. This was the door I had been waiting for all my life; I was about to enter my own Narnia.

The owner opened the door and switched on his torch. There were no fur coats to push past, but we stepped onto a wooden floor which was covered from floor to ceiling with cardboard boxes. 'They're not heavy,' said the owner, 'they've only got coat hangers in them, just push them out of the way.' So I did. By torchlight, we spent a good five minutes pushing the piles of boxes around until we had cleared a path through to the edge of the floor. I walked across to where a large timber roof truss erupted from the floor below, as if the roof of another building was trying to break through. The owner then handed me the torch, and with that thin golden beam, I picked out a scene that I could never have imagined still existed.

I could see that the alien roof truss was pushing through the front of a wooden balcony of partitioned bench seating which curved round like a horseshoe in front of me. It reminded me of a gallery in one of the larger Victorian churches. Large, boarded-up, arched windows flanked either side of the balcony and an arcaded ceiling loomed high above the intrusive timber truss. As I adjusted to the geography of the room, I realised that the invading structure was supporting the ceiling of the room below, the same ceiling which I had stood beneath and wondered about when the Leather Club was still trading. My torch beam traced across the ceiling above me, picking out the dirty-gold and brown colour scheme, stained with the tobacco smoke of the last paying audiences. In areas where the dirty gold had peeled off, other layers of decoration were revealed; dark blue with gold stars, pale blue, white and a layer of deep, sumptuous red. The centre of the ceiling was a lattice of wood and mesh with four portholes cut into

View of the balcony and the roof truss from the stage area

it where some form of lighting, probably gasoliers, must have once hung. At the back of the auditorium I could make out a projection room, one of the only twentieth-century alterations from a time when the music hall had been used as a cinema. To the right of the projection room was a large set of doors with the word 'Exit' above and a sign reading 'Gents' to the right of that.

I was stunned. Everything seemed to be here. I could almost hear the old audience shouting and booing at the act, thick tobacco smoke hanging in grey streamers above their heads. I got a sense of the overwhelming closeness, even in the icy chill of that February day. It was as if time had stood completely still in this place, as if someone had locked the door in 1938 and nothing, not even the air, had moved since.

Sign near the projection room

3 THE GENESIS OF GLASGOW ENTERTAINMENTS

To be one of the only people to witness this secret gem, hidden above what was now an amusement arcade, was an honour as unexpected as the building's survival. How could this magical little place have been left so forgotten? There was a real sense of abandonment about the place and I was determined to somehow enable it to feel the warmth of love and attention again. I knew that a handful of others had tried before me to get in, but few had got past the owners. I was the first to succeed where these others had failed and it was the beginning of the greatest adventure of my life.

I didn't need anyone to tell me how special this building was: the walls seeped history. The auditorium had come into use when children were still being shoved up chimneys and Charles Dickens was writing about the grim realties of life in Britain. Its history spanned the years to a time when motor cars and air travel were still in their infancy, before notions of class equality and the sexual revolution.

The footprint of the building itself, however, is believed to date back to a time even before that. Some time in the middle of the eighteenth century, it was a warehouse. In the 1700s, the tobacco lords had promenaded around the area in scarlet cloaks and tricorn hats, carrying silver-capped canes. It was they who covered the Trongate with large granite paving slabs, known as 'plane stanes', creating the first fully paved street of the city. And as they had paid for it, only they could enjoy the feel of firm granite beneath their well-heeled feet. Peasants were left to trudge through the cart-churned mud, and were likely to get punished for daring to step upon the hallowed plane stanes. That punishment would generally be a quick crack of a tobacco lord's cane against the shin, but if the offence was repeated, the merchant had every right to take the punishment further and have the culprit lug-pinned at the Tolbooth. This delightful practice involved nailing the ear of the criminal to the door of the Tolbooth using a hand-hammered, flat-headed nail. The victim was then left to tear themselves free. In Glasgow this rather brutal punishment of minor offences was regarded as entertainment. In fact when the practice was banned in the 1830s, it was not because of the cruelty of the punishment, but rather (according to the burgh records) because it 'corrupted Community life'. In order to cheer on the lug-pinned victim, 'weavers would leave their looms and children play truant'. Well, at that time entertainments were not so easy to come by. Theatre was not legitimised in Glasgow until the mid eighteenth century as, until then, it was regarded, by the pious population of the city, as the work of the devil.

From the 1730s, travelling minstrels had to come to Glasgow, generally performing in the hall of Daniel Booth, a dancing master, as they were not permitted to perform in the street. By the 1740s other places began to provide amusements; entertainments of all sorts, especially novelties, began to spring up in various quarters, particularly in the East End near Glasgow Green and Glasgow Cross. Amongst the most popular novelties were animal acts like dancing bears and acrobatic performing fleas. The *Glasgow Mercury* in 1787 advertised a '"Learned Pig", a most singular phenomenon' which was exhibited by a Mr Nicholson, a man 'possessed of an exclusive and peculiar power over the most irrational part of animated nature'. In other words, he had managed to teach a rather bizarre collection of animals to perform a variety of tricks: he had, apparently, trained a turtle to fetch and carry objects, a hare to beat a drum, turkey cocks to country dance and 'three cats to strike several tunes on the dulcimer with their paws, and to imitate the Italian manner of singing'. His greatest achievement, however, was 'conquering the natural obstinacy and stupidity of a pig, by teaching him to unite the letters of any person's name, to tell the number of persons present in the room and the hour and minute by any watch'. 'This singular creature', it was claimed, 'may justly be deemed the greatest curiosity in the kingdom . . .'

A 'learned pig' of such talent today would perhaps still draw a curious audience, but one popular act from the past which people would recoil from today definitely is the flea circus. The very thought makes me itch, but I do find the idea fascinating. Flea circuses were hugely popular. Miniature sets were created for the flea to perform in: tiny furnishings, tricks and routines were set up and the audience would watch as the props spun, swung and rolled. The most wonderful description of a flea circus was featured as an advertisement in the *Glasgow Journal* in 1763. It describes the collection of miniature 'curiosities' which could be viewed at the

Mason's Arms, Trongate, and included

> An Ivory chaise with four wheels, and all the proper apparatus belonging to them, turning readily on their axis together with a man sitting on the chaise, all drawn by a flea, without any seeming difficulty, the chaisemen and flea being barely equal to a single grain.
>
> A flea chained to a chain of 200 links, with a padlock and key – all weighing less than one third of a grain. The padlock locks and unlocks . . .
>
> A landau, which opens and shuts by springs, hanging on braces, with four persons therein, two footmen behind, a coachman on the box with a dog between his legs, six horses and a postilion, all drawn by a single flea!

All this for only one shilling!

The owner of this particular flea circus was one Mr S. Boverick and he drew quite an audience for his shows, which could be viewed daily from nine in the morning till eight in the evening. There is some debate as to whether these shows did use real performing fleas or were just little tricks set up by the ringmaster himself. I will leave you to make up your own mind. Certainly Mr Boverick's advertising attracted a rather large queue outside the Mason's Arms, the assembled people drawing the attention of a lady who was passing by on her way home.

The lady had come to Glasgow to sell her produce at the market and, upon seeing the crowd, decided to investigate. After waiting in the queue, she paid her shilling and entered the Mason's Arms where the event was located. The room was very grand, with high ceilings, long velvet drapes and plush furnishings. Situated on a table in the middle of the room was the collection of wonderful novelties and magnifying glasses so that the visitor might more easily view them. Mr Boverick then began the show and a tiny flea began to pull the miniscule chaise.

The lady joined the other visitors and was inspecting the tiny props with a magnifying glass when suddenly she noticed the flea. It was probably quite a shock to see one so magnified. She was so appalled at the filthy beast being present in such grand surroundings, that she crushed it with her thumbnail, unaware that this little creature was what she had paid to see performing. S. Boverick was horrified; this had been his favourite flea, which he had kept in a silk-lined box and fed from the blood of his own arm. He considered taking the woman to court, but as she was a widow with very little in the way of worldly possessions, he decided to cut his losses and train a new educated flea.

The range of entertainments available from the mid 1700s prompted the building of Glasgow's first theatre, which was rather audaciously erected against the wall of the bishop's palace, near the cathedral. It was a primitive wooden shack, rather hastily erected and sadly not destined to endure for long. It opened as the Castle Yard Booth, (sometime between 1752 and 1754) but no sooner had it been built than the followers of the rather militant Reverend George Whitfield declared it a 'Den of Iniquity' and burned it to the ground.

Although he preached against the immoral practices and evils surely inherent in the theatrical arts and those that practised them, Whitfield was, ironically, a great showman himself. His presence in the pulpit was formidable and he was famed for his ability to enflame his parishioners with his passionate sermons. His sermons in the cathedral burial ground raised money for the poor and also raised £60 towards the erection of the Black Bull Inn (where Robert Burns frequently stayed when visiting Glasgow as a Customs and Excise man). It is also ironic to think that the reason for the religious opposition to the theatre was on the grounds that it endangered the spiritual and moral well-being of the populace who were, apparently, always mortally in danger of the temptations of the flesh. This nanny culture thought it far healthier for the public to spend what leisure time they had watching public punishments and attending executions. (The latter gained the greatest audience; the last public hanging, for example, highly publicised as a family day out, attracted nearly 100,000 spectators on Glasgow Green.) Fortunately leisure time was a rare luxury, except for on Sundays, and even then the whole population of the city would cram into the churches around the city. For the benefit of their immortal souls, attendance at church was compulsory.

In 1764 an attempt was made to build another theatre for Glasgow, and erring on the side of caution, this theatre was built on the outskirts of the city where, technically, it wasn't in Glasgow at all. The Alston Theatre was opened in the village of Grahamston, then just to the west of the city, although now a part of the city centre – the village is buried beneath Central Station. This controversial little theatre didn't get off to the best of starts either. The land on which the Alston stood had been sold to the theatre company by John Miller of Westerton. As the theatre was being built, the religious zealots were already vowing to ensure that it would not open. As the opening night approached, notices advertising the event began to appear, alerting the public to the impending theatrical entertainment. On the opening night, a group of angry protesters gathered at nearby Anderson Cross, and, armed only with their piety and a few well-chosen weapons, they set off in a torch-lit procession to disrupt the performance. They were led by a preacher who declared that he had dreamt of being in hell, where the devil himself had raised a toast to Mr Miller for selling the land for the 'Deil's ain hoose'. By the time the protestors arrived at the Alston they were fuelled to a zealous fever pitch and attempted to burn the devil out of his house. Fortunately the flames were easily doused by those who did not share their violent hatred of entertainment. Many local men and women gathered together and helped to clear up the damage. Even the opening star herself, Mrs Bellamy, gave a substantial donation and encouraged some of the more liberal-minded worthies of the city to do the same, raising a total of £400 in the process. A temporary stage was erected and the first show, a play called *The Citizen*, was shortly followed by *The Farce of the Mock Doctor*.

Like the Castle Yard Booth, though, this little theatre was not to be long-lived, for only a few years later, in May 1780, a mysterious fire burned down the wooden building. When the firemen turned up to douse the flames, a magistrate proclaimed, 'Save the ither folk's hooses an' let the De'il's hoose burn.' But it was too late for religious prohibition: public opinion was being swayed in favour of the theatre, which was fast becoming a popular escape from the struggle of every day life. Although it still wasn't (and wouldn't be for a long time) wholly accepted, theatre became more tolerated, the church quieting its protests, unable to fight against the public's desire for frivolity.

The Dunlop Street theatre opened in 1782. It cost £3,000 to build, and, once completed, it boasted entertainment spread over two floors. As soon as the doors opened the public streamed in, and the building was always full to bursting. However, by 1822 or so, the Dunlop Street theatre had come upon hard times. It was now an old theatre which was shabby and uncomfortable compared with the sumptuous new Theatre Royal on Queen Street, which stole the lion's share of the audiences. The Dunlop Street theatre's lease became available, attracting the attention of two rival actor-managers. Both approached the vendor, struck a deal and parted with money.

The two new owners arrived at the premises to make ready their new purchase, but when they saw each other, they at once began to bicker. The

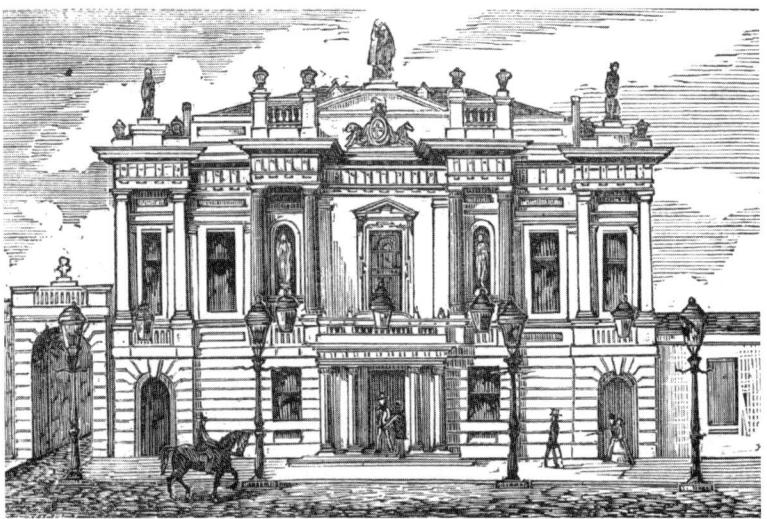

The theatre on Dunlop Street

bickering became a fight and magistrates were called in to settle the dispute. The magistrate decided that they were both entitled to use the premises and since the theatre had two floors, it was settled that they should share the building. So Mr Seymour took the upper section of the building which still contained a working auditorium, and J.H. Alexander contented himself with the lower portion which had once functioned as an auditorium, but in recent years had been used by a potato salesman and a cotton dealer for storage. Alexander must have felt very hard done by as he strived to make ready his basement theatre and clear away the smell and muck left behind by tons of mouldy spuds.

It wasn't long before the Dunlop Street theatre was reopened under its new management and two new names. Downstairs, Alexander had given his venue the whimsical title of Dominion of Fancy, whilst upstairs Mr Seymour opened his Caledonian Theatre. It seemed that the dispute had been amicably settled. However, the battle had not yet begun. On opening night, upstairs in the Caledonian, Seymour and his cast were dramatising the famous Shakespearian play *Macbeth*, whilst downstairs in the Dominion, Alexander was regaling his audience with a particularly noisy version of the Battle of Inch. The raucous battle-scenes downstairs (which were also accompanied by flashes of blue flame that flared through the stage-boards above) disrupted the performance of *Macbeth* above.

The audience upstairs, unable to enjoy the performance they had paid good money to see, protested loudly. Seymour, infuriated by this disruption to his play, stormed downstairs and punched Alexander on the nose. War was declared between the two managers and the pair began to fight it out with members of the audiences joining in.

The magistrates were again called in and it was decreed that the managers should open their theatres on separate nights; Seymour was given Tuesday to Friday and Alexander Saturday to Monday. This did not suit Seymour as Saturday and Monday were the busiest days of the week, so, when it was Alexander's turn to open, Seymour arranged a private party, complete with a brass band, to ensure that the entertainments downstairs were thoroughly disrupted. He also lifted the floorboards and poured water – and I don't mean nice clean tap water – onto the audience below.

Alexander was not pleased, but rather than respond with another fist fight, he decided to hit Seymour where it would do the most damage, and made plans to poach his audience. On the following Tuesday, Seymour advertised the following week's play for the Caledonian, a German piece entitled *Der Freischütz*. Alexander did the same and his adaptation began its three-night run the Saturday prior to Seymour's opening night. Alexander packed them in with the promise of a real fire-breathing dragon. Halfway through the play, the promised dragon waddled onto the stage belching fire at the audience. Suddenly, from above, an actor appeared, dangling by his ankles from the theatre upstairs. He grabbed the dragon by its tail and prevented it from leaving the stage and extinguishing its flames. The threat of fire in the wooden auditorium sent the audience and actors into panic and they fled from the building. The dangling actor released the dragon (which was then able to douse itself) and Seymour and his gang pulled their champion back up.

Seymour next advertised a piece entitled *Tom and Jerry*, which Alexander duly presented first. This time, however, both houses were packed to bursting every night as the battle of the two managers had become the talk of the town, attracting the biggest crowds the little theatre had ever seen. Of course, this now meant that the Theatre Royal on Queen Street was considerably down on its takings. The manager, who was now struggling with mounting debts, decided to place the building on the market. Seymour, who had become thoroughly sick of his rival, sold his share in the Dunlop Street Theatre for £6,000 to Alexander and moved in to the Theatre Royal.

This tale is quite comical and worthy of becoming a comedy sketch in its own right, but the Dunlop Street Theatre was also the site of one of the worst theatre disasters in Glasgow's history. On Saturday 17 February 1849, during the second act of *Surrender of Calais*, someone in the gallery made a false cry of 'Fire!' Fire was a hazard of these old wooden auditoriums which relied on limelight, coal fires and gas lighting. The audience panicked and a terrible scene followed as people desperately scrambled over each other to get out of the dangerous burning building. Sixty-five people were trampled to death.

By now, theatre, travelling shows, poets' boxes, street hawkers and ballad criers had become a part of everyday life in Glasgow, especially around the Saltmarket, Glasgow Cross and Glasgow Green. Traditionally the travelling shows came to the city for the two-week Glasgow Fair. During the fair, temporary booths would be erected around the Green, offering the public a variety of entertainments. The booths, or 'geggies' as they were known, were made of timber and canvas and were designed to be quickly erected and dismantled. Managed by travelling showmen or actors who were in-between theatre engagements, these simple structures generally held up to 400 people, but some of these temporary booths weren't quite so temporary and became features of the city long after the annual fair had finished. The Adelphi (1842) and the City Theatre (1845) were both of a more substantial build, with brick included in their construction. The City Theatre could hold 3,000 people, and it did so almost continuously. The entertainments on view were crafted for a viewing audience which had been weaned on public punishments and executions: magic acts, tumblers, jugglers, performing animals, novelties and melodramas were the main bill of fare. Although only a few minutes in length, the melodramas contained several acts which would always be action-packed with fights, damsels in distress and dastardly villains. Anything of a Scottish nature was obviously popular, particularly if it involved fighting. Blood, guts, heroism and villainy were essential elements in attracting the paying public.

Plays by Shakespeare were also a popular attraction, albeit in a seriously abridged form comprising chiefly the most violent or tragic parts. One geggy, for example, offered *Richard III* in five acts 20 times in seven hours! Another house advertised the death scenes from *Romeo and Juliet*, and after each performance the crowd cried 'Again! Again!'

Visitors to the fair wanted to be horrified, amused and distracted, which

Geggies erected on the edge of Glasgow Green during the Glasgow Fair, 1825

meant the novelties received as much custom as the melodramas. One which is often referred to in the archives is the exhibition of two primitive tribesmen from Africa who terrified the audience by acting in a savage manner, roaring fiercely at the audience and shouting in a primitive language. They would finish their act by tearing apart a rat with their teeth and then eating it. Not everyone who saw this act was convinced that the tribesmen were in fact from Africa: it was rumoured that they were Irish workers dressed in rabbit skins and covered in boot-black or soot and that the 'primitive' language they spoke was in fact Gaelic. Whatever the truth was, this act, billed as 'The Bosjesmans' attracted over 90,000 visitors!

The temporary and semi-permanent structures on the Green were stiff competition for the permanent, legitimate theatres, which paid hefty licence fees. The protests from the theatre managers forced the geggies out, so they relocated to Vinegar Hill, where the travelling show-people can still be found today.

By this time, Glasgow had changed. King George III had lost the American colonies and the tobacco trade with Virginia was severed, leaving the wealthy tobacco lords teetering on the verge of bankruptcy. It was lucky for Glasgow that living on the Trongate was a young lad from Greenock called James Watt. His modifications to Thomas Newcomen's engine were to help catapult Britain into the industrial age and place Glasgow at its heart. Ideally located geologically for the mining of essential mineral resources such as coal and iron ore, and with the river Clyde feeding it, Glasgow quickly became an industrial centre which needed a workforce. Across Britain, cottage industries had begun to crumble in the wake of mass production and thousands of men became desperate for work. Immigrants flooded in from the Highlands and islands of Scotland, as well as from Ireland and the north of England. During the height of the Potato Famine in Ireland, over 1,000 Irish arrived at the Broomielaw Quay every week. They all came to find work and all needed accommodation. The city did what it could to provide the population with adequate housing, but space was at a premium as hundreds of thousands of people attempted to squash themselves into a few ancient, already crumbling streets. The 'single end' lifestyle became commonplace.

A single end was basically the Victorian equivalent of a modern bedsit, with living, sleeping and cooking areas in one room and shared toilet facilities outside. Whole families, and sometimes more than one family, would often live in a single end. Human waste was simply thrown into open drains, the cramped and unsanitary conditions adding disease to an already difficult, dismal and hard life.

Thousands of workers toiled in the dangerous working conditions of the factories, mills, mines and shipyards, forging a reputation for the city as centre of industrial prowess and gaining Glasgow the title 'Workshop of the World'. It was a title that the city fathers were proud to wear. For the working man, however, it meant labouring at least ten hours a day, six days a week, earning about 3 shillings 6d a day (minus fines for late attendance, slovenly work, accidents and anything else the mill owner could think of to reduce his wages bill). At the end of the week, workers at the factories, mills and shipyards would spill out of their workplaces and into the many pubs which had opened to slake the working man and woman's thirst. And it was in the pubs that the history of music hall was founded.

Entertainment has been found in taverns since the first alcoholic beverage was served in one. The good old pub sing-along has existed for centuries, but in the middle of the nineteenth century landlords and landladies began to make special provisions for this ad hoc entertainment by providing a back room containing a platform, a piano and a chairman to introduce the 'turns' and preside over the activities. These places became known as 'Free and Easies' and were the preferred resort of the ordinary populace in the 1830s and 1840s.

The legitimate theatres complained bitterly when their ticket-paying audience began to abandon them for these free amateur shows. The geggies were bad enough, but at least they presented shows with some worthy content and used professional performers. These tavern entertainments on the other hand were, they argued, a free-for-all which encouraged immoral behaviour. In 1843, prompted by the growing number of Free and Easies in the industrial cities across Britain, a new Theatre Act was passed which ordered that these places should be properly licensed, and therefore easier to regulate. Or so you would think. When the first legitimate music halls or singing saloons began to spring up, they were more or less just an extension of their unlicensed predecessors, only with more professional acts on the bill.

They were also rough places and not for the faint-hearted, although they were not solely for the working classes; some of the wealthier men of the city frequented them when they sought an unusual and slightly bawdier night out. The audience regularly got out of control and the chairman would spend much of his time bringing them back into order, like a judge presiding over an unruly court, frequently banging a gavel and shouting, 'Order!' The chairman would also be expected to do a turn himself if they were short on performers or if the audience demanded it. The roughest houses had barriers between the audience and the stage to prevent the less gentlemanly spectators from attempting to climb onto the stage and becoming too friendly with the ladies performing there. By the 1850s, Glasgow's East End, now the habitual haunt for fun-seekers, boasted several music halls. They were a brightly lit contrast to the dark lives of the audience.

How the Trongate had changed. Less than a hundred years earlier Daniel Defoe had described this area of the city as 'the beautifullest little city in Europe'. By now, though, the Trongate was a stretch of depravity and squalor, with over 200 brothels and 100 or more shebeens – illegal drinking houses. In the Laigh Kirk close (an early version of a block of council flats) at 59 Trongate, there were six brothels and four shebeens.

Businesses were rapidly moving to more prosperous areas as the city extended westwards and commercial buildings in the East End became empty. One such deserted building was an old warehouse in the Trongate, which had previously been a blacking manufacturer's and a spirit dealer's premises. It was left to the architect Thomas Gildard and his partner Robert H.M. MacFarlane to find a new and sustainable use for it.

4 GILDARD AND MACFARLANE: THE BUILDING OF BRITANNIA

Thomas Gildard was born on 20 May 1822. His parents were English, his father a prosperous hotelier. However, a life in hospitality was not for young Tom. In 1838 he was apprenticed to David and James Hamilton, notable architects of Glasgow, where Thomas was to train with a couple of other youngsters who would themselves leave a mark on Glasgow's architectural heritage: John Thomas Rochead, who later designed the Wallace Monument, and Charles Wilson, whose elegant buildings can be seen across the city.

In about 1852, Thomas Gildard started in partnership with another young architect, Robert H.M. MacFarlane. When Gildard and MacFarlane were first invited to look at an old warehouse on the Trongate, their plan was to replace the front of the plain building with something a little more suited to Glasgow's position as the second city of the Empire. This was an opportunity to show the world their talent as architects and they would certainly make the best of it. By the end of the summer of 1857 a temple to classical design had appeared, complete with cherubs, carved swags, arched windows, Grecian key decoration and the inscription MDCCCLVII (1857) carved into the stone beneath the apex.

It was an elegant and prominent front for the activities that would go on behind it. Generally music halls were located up alleys and backstreets, but this building had a very prominent main-street frontage. But then, Gildard and MacFarlane had not set out to create a music hall. In fact, it seems that the original brief might well have been to create a department store, where all manner of commodities could be purchased under the one roof – the latest mode in shopping for a class of patron who could afford to be modern. The Trongate, however, was populated by bare-footed children, gin-soaked prostitutes and honest but desperately poor East-End citizens. At some stage in the construction of the building, it seems it was decided that a department store would be of no use in a part of town where the

Thomas Gildard

wealthier ladies of the city dared not tread. Instead, the building would become something of worth for the local population: a music hall.

This sudden change in end use meant the internal structure of the building would need a completely different approach. While a department store would have showroom floors on which to display goods and allow the shopper to browse at leisure, a music hall required enough space to accommodate an audience and a stage for the performances. As a result, the layout of the hall was very basic, its design dependent on whatever materials were available on quick demand. At the time there were a lot of churches being built to support the new and burgeoning congregations, and it is likely that materials were occasionally 'borrowed' or purchased from these other construction sites, along with some of the workmen.

The horseshoe balcony (which was cut into an original show-room floor of the old warehouse) had been designed to hold as many standing souls as possible. Ship builders had been employed to help fit out and furnish the auditorium and they left their mark with the techniques used to provide the balcony and its huge, curved supporting beams. The balcony's simple spike-nailed construction meant it sagged dangerously when full to capacity, which it undoubtedly was for the majority of the shows.

The final result was an auditorium, the facilities of which were basic and functional. The construction was almost entirely of wood. A simple platform served as a stage for the entertainments whilst the audience were provided with seats in the stalls – the lower portion of the hall – and standing accommodation at the back and in the balcony. There were no toilets, bar, disabled access, changing rooms, fire exits nor any of the other facilities we expect today.

The horseshoe balcony

The decoration, however, was a different matter and continued the grand classical theme of the facade with beautifully moulded cornicing and expertly stencilled acanthus leaf decoration in soft terracotta and buff tones. The quality and elegance of the décor rivalled that of the bigger, plusher legitimate theatres and halls, whilst the overall impact of the high ceiling and wooden, petitioned gallery gave the design a distinctly clerical flavour – the 'hoose o the De'il' modelled on the House of God. What makes this even more ironic is that a year after completing the Britannia Music Hall, Gildard delivered a paper in which he condemned the church architecture then being built, particularly the Gothic designs, which he described as 'the vanity of individuals and the pride of congregations': two of the seven deadly sins, literally set in stone. Whatever Gildard felt about the kind of place of amusement his Trongate building was providing for the public is hard to say. Certainly he was a devout man, but he also loved his city and believed in providing what was most useful for the local population. Whether or not Gildard and MacFarlane had begun with a music hall in mind, the result was one which today is regarded as a fine example of its type.

It seems that the relationship between the two young architects was very close and was further strengthened when MacFarlane fell in love with and married Gildard's sister, Eliza Taylor Gildard. Tragically, the marriage was cut short when poor Eliza died quite suddenly. This tragedy was to affect MacFarlane so strongly that his own health began to suffer. He gradually drew away from society and Gildard became his only contact with the outside world. With his spirit and heart broken, MacFarlane finally died of consumption in 1862, alone in his house in the west end of the city. His body was discovered by Gildard, who was now left to grieve his best friend as well as his sister.

The partnership of Gildard and MacFarlane is only remembered for two commissions, Britannia Music Hall and 1–8 Belhaven Terrace on Great Western Road. Gildard was still a young man with much of his life ahead of him and two well-regarded designs behind him. Whether or not he tried to find a suitable replacement for his brother-in-law is not known, but soon after the end of his partnership with MacFarlane, Thomas joined the council's Department of Works.

He was to spend much of his career there working with two other distinguished architects of the city, John Carrick and A.B. MacDonald. This was the most exciting time to be an architect; the city was growing and expanding at such a rate that new buildings seemed to appear daily. New streets opened, lined with the latest fashions in architecture, and old streets were remodelled, replacing the ancient, ramshackle wrecks that remained in the older parts of town with gleaming new buildings. Architects were also encouraging some of the greatest designers Scotland would know. Modern design drew its influence from the elegant, classical styles of the past, a mode which was lead by Alexander 'Greek' Thomson. Gildard had been friends with Thomson since his apprenticeship with the Hamiltons, and in fact Thomson's influence can be seen in the design of Britannia Music Hall.

Although during his time working for the city Gildard worked with many noteworthy architects, he respected Alexander Thomson above all others, declaring him in one article to be 'the unknown genius'. Gildard wrote dozens of articles in his life for a variety of London and Scottish journals; in fact, he is better known for his writing than he is for his buildings. His ability as an architectural commentator was to gain him a well-deserved place in the city's history books. Many of the articles penned by Gildard remain as a valuable legacy, with rich and colourful descriptions of the Glasgow of his youth and the buildings which he saw replace the streetscape of his boyhood. They also provide an insight into the personalities which inhabited the nineteenth century world of architecture, building and design. Even in his lifetime, Gildard's commentaries were described as a link between present and past generations.

In the last years of his life Gildard became one of the most noted senior gentlemen of the city. A piece published in *The Bailie* on 12 June 1889 gives perhaps the finest contemporary description of him:

> One of the best-known figures in the Glasgow of to-day is that of Mr Thomas Gildard of the office of Public Works. Tall and spare, with well-cut, regular features, his brow crowned with a wealth of silvery locks, Mr Gildard possesses an air at once of culture and of distinction. Some of this air belongs to his profession of architect and some of it to his own personality. Shy and self-absorbed among strangers, when in the company of those whom he knows and likes, Mr Gildard is cheery and chatty to a degree. A keen observer, and owning a wonderfully retentive memory, his conversation is always interesting, whether it turns on books or on men.

In December 1895 Thomas Gildard died. His best-known architectural achievement, the Britannia Music Hall, was, however, in its prime.

 THE EARLY DAYS OF BRITANNIA

When Gildard and MacFarlane's theatre first opened, it appears to have been called Willie Campbell's Singing Saloon. Within a few months, though, John Brand took over the building and renamed it Britannia Music Hall, the name inspired by the statue of Britannia which was, until 1949, a local landmark at Glasgow Cross and was easily viewed from the front doors of the music hall.

At first Britannia had no licence for the sale of alcohol. Nor did it have any connection to a pub. It quickly gained the reputation of being a 'dry house', sending hoards of drink-loving patrons through the doors of less sober premises. A notice was soon put on the wall advertising the Ship Tavern, '200 yards to the left-hand side'. Soon after, a pub, the Britannia Vaults, opened on the ground floor and the patrons came flooding in.

The early audiences were predominantly male – it was not deemed the sort of place that ladies of any respectability should frequent, and, in any case, many women not only worked, but also had their hands full cooking, cleaning and looking after their large broods of children: eight or ten children in a family was not uncommon.

Painted notice for the Ship Tavern

The Britannia was somewhere men could find a bit of titillation and blow off a little steam. Victorian morality dictated that women covered themselves from the neck to the floor. Those women who exposed flesh were regarded as harlots, and so not much flesh was generally on view in public life – except in the music hall, where dancing girls and lady acrobats would expose legs in costumes skimpy by Victorian standards. This sort of risqué entertainment gave the lady performers an opportunity to make a shilling or two, and soliciting became a problem in music halls, with Britannia being no exception.

Prostitution has always been a precarious occupation; soliciting on the streets ran the risk of a beating and a night in the police cells, whilst the dark lanes and backstreets left the women exposed to mortal peril. The dark corners of the crowded music halls, however, offered the working girls a relatively safe environment, warm and dry, and with plenty of entertainment to distract the crowd as they plied their trade.

The biggest fear of the pious population had been realised. However, morality and decency were not exclusive to the middle and upper classes. The poorest too expected a certain standard of morality. In fact, it was about the only expectancy they had. A wife wanted her husband to come home at night sober and free of disease, yet everybody who strived for a decent life at least deserved decent entertainment at the end of the day.

John Brand was not blind to the public's misgivings and took steps to create an environment which was comfortable, wholesome and safe (to an extent) for the whole family. In the early 1860s he invested some money in upgrading the Britannia so that it would be more comfortable and enticing to the family audience and more able to compete with the grander music halls which were then starting to appear. In the balcony, which had originally been standing-room only, he added long, wooden pews and above the stage he added a proscenium arch.

Brand's alterations were completed in a manner indicative of the original fit-out of the auditorium. The pews were probably reclaimed and the proscenium was made out of old bits of timber which had either been lying around or rescued from some other building, then nailed together and covered (on the auditorium side) with canvas which was painted and decorated in a fancy manner. Only the performers saw the rough edges; to the public, it was a richly decorated frame for the antics on stage.

Once a more comfortable environment had been achieved, it was time to tackle the 'wholesome' aspect of the place, which meant taking measures to cut down the amount of prostitutes who used the building as their main place of business. Brand employed a strict door policy and began printing the disclaimer 'no ladies admitted unless accompanied by gentlemen' on all his bills. It seems that once banned from selling their wares in Britannia, those plucky prostitutes moved across the road where they opened a small brothel; they would then find their 'gentleman' before they entered the hall. Many a fly button was left beneath the balcony pews, perhaps as a testament to this occupation, and years later, buried among the buttons, was found a card advertising 'Dr Temple for diseases peculiar to men'.

The Britannia's notoriety for the ladies of the night was a source of comic comment in the local theatrical press, with anecdotes such as this one appearing in 1883 in *Barr's Professional Gazette*:

> A masher [toff] led his best girl into the Britannia Music Hall and paid the modest amount of threepence per head. Two youngsters sat down and one said to the other, 'Man, Jock, if I wis gaun' wi' a judy [prostitute], I'd think shame tae tak' her intae the 3d seats, wid you no?' The masher and his girl heard the remark and disappeared before the performance was far advanced.

By now, music hall was a family treat. Up to 1,500 people would pile into Britannia for every show, which ran as many as four times a day. Glasgow's hardest working and poorest population squeezed themselves next to others on the wooden benches, with not a hair's breadth between them, and waited for the show to start. Clutching their pokes [bags] of mouldy vegetables, which they could buy from the vegetable seller who sold his rotten stock from a barrow in the lane, they sat together in a great human herd, munching and mooing in the gas-lit dimness as they drank their beer and prised steaming whelks (the first popular take-away food) from their shells. The atmosphere was thick with Woodbine smoke and the smell of people – this was prior to the invention of deodorant and luxury of indoor plumbing. The noise, the smell, the press of the crowd, the cries of babies and the heat from the open fires were a heady concoction. It was hardly a relaxing or comfortable environment.

When 1,500 people were crammed together like that, mob mentality was easily triggered. If one person didn't, for some reason, like the act and began demonstrating their displeasure, a ripple of dissatisfaction would spread through the swell of humanity like a Mexican wave. Before long, a perpetual shower of rivet punchings, rotten cabbage and whelk shells, along with a cacophony of verbal abuse, would come hailing down upon the poor supplicant on stage. This behaviour gained the early music-hall audience a reputation for leaving 'no turn un-stoned'.

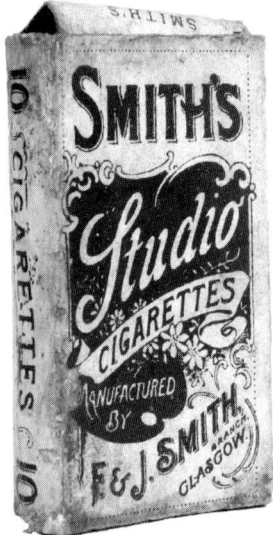 

Victorian cigarette packets found in Britannia

But it wasn't just the shower of objects that caused problems; smoking was also a source of discomfort for the erstwhile performer. In one report, the smoking in Britannia had become such a problem that there was a call for its ban – not because of any health reasons you understand; at this time smoking was considered good for the health (which is perhaps a contributing factor to why the average life span was only 45 years) – no, the complaint came from a performer who claimed that he couldn't see the audience and the audience could not see him because the cloud of smoke was so thick.

⑥ JOHN BRAND PROUDLY PRESENTS

DAN LENO: THE FUNNIEST MAN ON EARTH

During the first couple of decades, amongst the most popular entertainments in Britannia were singers (Irish songs being very popular because of the large Irish population in the area), dancers, clog dancers and comics. The comedians of this time were quite far removed from the stand-up comics of today. At this time they used comedy characterisations and funny songs to poke fun at the famous people of the time and common situations. Swearing was not accepted on the public stage, and, although some of the material was often regarded as saucy or close to the bone, the majority of it was about as offensive as a Christmas cracker joke.

John Brand knew what his audience wanted and provided it in abundance. He always strove to put the best he could book on the bill and followed the popular trends of the day. It was during his reign, in 1866, that Dan Leno, a young lad – only five years old at the time – performed at the Britannia. He had in fact already been wowing and wooing audiences for over a year. His cute posturing and nimble little feet subsequently carried him on a career path which saw him grow up (to a diminutive five foot three inches) in the limelight and become one of the most successful performers of his generation, with the name Dan Leno known in every household of Britain.

Dan's real name was George Wilde Galvin. He used to claim that he had been born under Platform 1 of St Pancras Station on 20 December 1860. He was, in reality, born in Eve Place, which sat beside the old Church of St Pancras until the site was brought by the Midland Railway Company and flattened to make way for the famous St Pancras Station.

George was the son of John Galvin, a performer who originally hailed from Ireland, and Louisa Dutton. They were both stage performers (he a comedian and she a vocalist) and had performed together for a number of years, billed as 'Mr & Mrs Johnny Wilde, the Singing and Acting Duettists'. Mr and Mrs Johnny Wilde managed to find almost constant work, but their combined wage was barely enough to feed, clothe and house the whole family. Like many families, they made do, and for the first few years of his life, George, who was and would always be the smallest of their four children, slept in a chest of drawers.

From the age of four George began performing on the professional stage. His first performance was at the Cosmotheca Music Hall in Paddington, London, where he was billed as 'Little George, the Infant Wonder, Contortionist and Posturer'. During his act the tiny lad would impersonate a corkscrew opening a bottle of wine to hoots of laughter and applause from the audience. He was an instant success, but alas these happy times were not to last: in 1864, tragedy struck when Johnny Galvin died. He was only 37, but his years of performing in the music halls, and the heavy drinking which often accompanied it, resulted in his early demise, leaving his wife and business partner a widow with four children, and little means to support them.

As a solo artiste Louisa struggled to keep enough money coming in and every night her little family watched her from the wings. Single women had a much tougher time at the hands of music-hall managers than their male counterparts and four shows a night barely brought in enough money to pay the rent. For several months she struggled as a single parent, until she found herself being courted by a fellow performer. When he asked her to marry him she could not afford to refuse, and so she became Mrs William Grant.

Grant performed under the stage name Dan Leno. Where the name Dan came from is not known, but he claimed that the name Leno was a reference to a city in Italy where he had had great success early on in his career. Like her first husband, Grant combined hard work with hard drink. He had originally come from Lancashire and had started his career touring the music halls in the north of England where he had enjoyed a fair degree of success. He thought, like hundreds of other performers, that stage work in London was plentiful and lucrative, and so moved to the capital. Like hundreds of others, he was disappointed. Now he was also confronted with the responsibility of providing for a wife and four children. He soon realised that life on the London stage would not support his new family and instead decided to move back to his home county of Lancashire. From here he hoped that he and his wife could found a new act and new reputation by travelling the halls in the north, where he had always been well received in the past. However, this new life of touring meant that it was not practical to cart around four children, so Louisa was forced to leave behind two of her brood, Henry and Frances, with her first husband's cousins, the Galvins. Only the talented little George and his older brother Jack joined their mother and stepfather.

Both children had performed on the stage before, so, rather than send the boys to work in one of the Lancashire mills, Grant decided to groom them for a new routine and gave Jack the task of teaching George how to dance. Before long they were billed as the 'Brothers Leno', which is how they were advertised when they performed with Louisa and William Grant (billed as 'Mr & Mrs Leno') in the Britannia in 1866.

Mr & Mrs Leno
The Unrivalled Characteristic Comic Duettists, Burlesque Actors, Dancers, &c.
Owing to their great success, they are engaged to appear at this establishment in 1867.
~
Thousands nightly are unable to gain admission to hear the PEOPLE'S FAVOURITE,
MR MOLLOY
The Great Irish Comic Vocalist, Dancer, and Reciter.
~
Last Week the[y] present the SUCCESSFUL ENGAGEMENT of those world-renowned Artistes,
THE BROS. NEMO
THE GREAT JAPANESE JUGGLERS
Who will introduce during the week, MANY FRESH NOVELTIES.
~
BROTHERS LENO
The Popular Great Little Dancers, Last Week of their Engagement.
~
Body of Hall 2d. On Saturday 3d. Front or Side Boxes 4d.
Concert commences each evening at 7; Saturdays at 6. Doors Open half-an-hour previous.
Ladies not admitted unless accompanied by Gentlemen.
Children Full-Price to all parts of the Hall.
No Pass Out Checks

As Mr and Mrs Leno, Louisa and William's new burlesque routines got off to a promising start, and the audience of the Britannia cheered their approval. But it was little George who would steal the show. He was always popular with the audience, endearing himself to everyone who saw him.

In Belfast in 1869 George had been seen by Charles Dickens, who was obviously also charmed by the little lad's talents. He even spoke to the young Leno after the act and told him, 'Good, little man: you'll make headway!' A prediction from such a great name of the day could not have failed to influence the lad.

His Belfast visit was a reminder of his father's Irish roots, and little George began to adopt an Irish brogue; for a short time he was billed as 'The Great Little Leno, the quintessence of Irish Comedians'. He was still only a child and the Irish act was popular in the halls he toured in the north of England. Encouraged by this success, Grant decided to try his stepson on the London stage, but the Irish angle wasn't to the Londoners' taste so George changed act again and this time was billed as 'Great Little Leno – Descriptive and Cockney Vocalist'. By now it was obvious that he was destined to be a star. He could dance, tumble, act and sing, all to raucous approval from the audiences that saw him. It was obvious he had outgrown the tuition of his brother Jack, who had lost his heart for the stage and decided instead to stay in London, where he got himself a job as a labourer.

Postcard of Dan Leno (bottom) with Herbert Campbell and Johnny Danvers

Jack was almost immediately replaced by one of his cousins, Johnny Danvers. Johnny and George, who was now known as Dan, were the same age and worked well together, becoming close friends for the rest of their lives. They were billed together up to the mid 1880s, although latterly Dan was billed as a solo act alongside his cousin.

One of Dan's greatest advantages was his small size, even as an adult. His stature as a performer, however, continued to grow long after he didn't. His act involved physical comedy routines of acrobatic flips, trips and tumbles that mesmerised the audiences watching. He had an astounding sense of rhythm and timing and an incredible energy on stage. His act was unique and other performers would congratulate him on his abilities. But it wasn't his comic talents that initially bought Dan Leno the greatest acclaim.

In the late 1870s a new trend was hitting the music-hall stages: clog dancing. Dan had encountered clog dancing for the first time a few years earlier and had appreciated the clever footwork. When another act suggested that his physical talents would translate well to the fast and precise routines of the dance, George decided to teach himself how to do it.

The art of clog dancing or 'clogging' as it is sometimes called, is believed to have developed in the cotton mills of Lancashire in the eighteenth century. The mill floors were kept wet to retain the high humidity needed for spinning cotton and so the workers preferred to wear wooden-soled 'clogs', rather than leather-soled shoes or boots. As they worked at their machines, the men would tap their wooden soles along to the mechanical rhythms around them. During breaks, they would stand in the mill courtyard and compete to see who had the quickest feet and the best rhythm patterns. It wasn't long before this simple entertainment made it to the stage and by the mid nineteenth century clog dancing championships began to take place.

In 1880 Dan Leno won his first competition for clog dancing in Wakefield. His prize was a small amount of cash and a leg of mutton. Although he was already gaining a reputation as a comic, he was encouraged by this first success as a clogger and entered another contest at the Princess's Music Hall in Leeds, where a gold and silver belt weighing 44.5 ounces, £50 and the title 'Clog Dancing Champion of the World' were on offer as the prize.

The judges sat under the stage throughout the contest so that they could more easily listen to the beats that thundered on the wooden boards above their heads. Dan danced his finest, his small clogged feet a blur as they furiously tapped out a selection of perfect rhythms. He in fact boasted that he could 'put more beats into sixteen bars of music than a drummer [could] with his drumsticks'. The competition was tough, not least because it had been rigged in favour of the two favourites, Tom Ward and Tom Robson, but Dan's complicated patterns and rhythms were obviously far beyond the skill the favourites displayed and he walked away with the first prize and the championship belt.

In Leno's first biography, J. 'Hickory' Wood describes the nimble clog-dancing routine: 'He danced on the stage; he danced on a pedestal; he danced on a slab of slate; he was encored over and over again . . .'

Hot on the heels of the world championship title, Dan toured the music halls in the north of England again. One of the music halls on this tour included a revisit to our own dear Britannia.

September 4th 1880
BRITANNIA MUSIC HALL
Pre-eminently the most popular place of Amusement.
EDWARDS AND ASHFORD
PREMIER VARIETY ENTERTAINERS
DAN LENO CHAMPION OF THE TERPSICHOREAN ARTS
BROTHERS WILKINSON 'The Millingar Boys'
And a host of fresh arrivals on Monday.

Clog dancing was a fairly new phenomenon in Britannia and Leno's routine was the only act of its type on the bill. His first visit to the venue when he was five had been a resounding success and his balletic clogging of 1880 was no different, the crowd happily clapping and stamping along to the rapid beats of his clog serenade.

In 1881 and 1882 he again competed for the world title and again he won. In 1883 Leno defended his title for a fourth time, but this time he lost and had to hand over the belt to a new champion. Dan himself may have been disappointed, but not as disappointed as the huge crowd that had cheered him on; they were so upset by the decision of the judges that they insisted on a rematch. For six nights the two champions danced it out, their faces never showing expression, their torsos upright and taut as their feet frantically and rhythmically thundered towards glory. At last Dan emerged victorious and the belt was again his. The only problem was, the chap from whom he had regained the title had lost (or pawned) the belt and a new one had to be ordered.

Clog dancing continued to be a regular feature on the bill at Britannia: the notable American clogger, John Williams, for example, performed at the music hall for a week in 1885, and was billed as 'the greatest Clog Dancer the world has ever seen'. He and Leno competed against each other

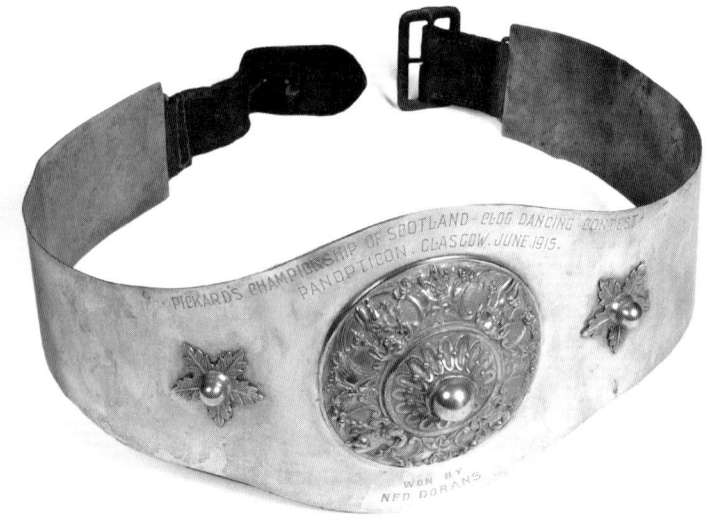

Silver champion's clogging belt

roughly a year later, the publicity leading up to the match implying a clash of the Titans rather than a mere dance-off. This was not so much a competition as a display of skills – Williams, like Leno, was also master of clogging.

In fact, perhaps thanks to the enthusiasm for clog dancing that Leno initially generated in the hall's audiences, the contests continued to amaze and entertain the Britannia crowds right into the twentieth century. Edward (Ned) Dorans won the impressive silver champion's belt in May 1914, which is now on display in the auditorium today after having been found in the Barras Market and gifted to the Britannia Panopticon trust by the Barras management in 1998. This 1914 competition, incidentally, was judged by a previous Britannia champion clog dancer, the Glaswegian J.G. Burns, who, despite having lost both legs when he had stepped into the path of a tram while on a visit to America (he had travelled across the Atlantic after having caught the attention of the silent movie business in Hollywood), had spent the rest of his career teaching the techniques of clog dancing with his hands.

It was whilst Dan was touring with his clog-dancing routine in 1883 that he found himself on the stage of a hall in Sunderland. On the bill was a young comedy vocalist by the name of Sarah Lydia Reynolds. Sarah was a sweet girl and made quite a stir with her slightly saucy act, which particularly affected young Dan who watched her with wide eyes from the wings. By the time he had finished his Sunderland engagement, he had fallen in love with Sarah and a year later they were married in St George's Church, Hulme, Manchester, with friends and family there to witness the nuptials. Dan was now doing well on the circuit, but was still not a high earner, so, instead of wedding cake, the couple offered their guests a cake-like confection made of bread and butter pudding, a good and stodgy start to their married life.

Soon after their wedding, the newly weds moved to London where Dan decided to return to his comic routines before his name had been completely forgotten by England's largest audience. Once he was back in his home town it seems that his career really took off. He was booked to play in three music halls a day, performing up to 20 times every day. Dan understood the low boredom threshold of the London crowd and so developed a whole gallery of characters which were well-observed caricatures of daily life: a beefeater showing visitors around the sights of the Tower of London, a Spanish bandit, a fire-fighter, a hairdresser, a policeman and a swimming master being among the most popular. He brought these caricatures to life through costume, dance and posturing, using a blend of songs and patter to give the character a voice. Take, for example, the swimming master. For this role he would wear a one-piece costume of knee-length shorts attached to a vest, made of horizontal striped material reminiscent of a deckchair. His knobbly knees, bow legs and mock sporty, manly gait, with shoulders back and chest puffed out, added to the comedy as he sang.

The Swimming Master

When the water is wet and the air is dry
A beautiful sight you may then espy
On the pier in the summer-time there am I
Teaching the ladies to swim.
Though frightened at first of the water they be,
Their confidence soon will return, don't you see
When they have feasted their eyes upon me
And noticed my figure so trim.

He would then break his singing for the patter:

You didn't notice my figure when I first appeared, I came on you too suddenly. You weren't able to grasp me altogether, as it were; I'll go off and come on again. *[Dan exits the stage and then re-enters.]* There! Now you can notice me properly. You see you've got a north-east view of me. It is really remarkable the effect I leave on people who see me for the first time. When I walked on the pier last Monday, two ladies looked at me and fell over into the water. I nearly got the Victoria Cross for that. Of course, that was my chance. The moment I saw the ladies in the water, quick as thought, I made one dash to where they tied the boat up; untied the boat, got in and pulled out. But I was just too late. The ladies could swim and they were saved. But it was a marvellous escape. If I'd saved them I'd have got the medal. I've nearly got twenty medals that way. I remember on another day something happened, just the same – only of course different. I nearly got another Victoria Medal! There was an old man, a very old man, all bearded and wrinkled, lying asleep on the sand. I was up on top, on the pr – pro – prom – on the pier. I dashed down before anybody could stop me, seized the old man, grabbed him by the legs, up on to the gravel and on to the pavement. Saved his life. There's not the slightest doubt if he had stayed there asleep till the tide come up, he'd have been drowned.

He would then continue singing:

As I teach the girls to float,
The sea goes down each throat.
They say, 'Oh Dear! I'm going to sink,'
I have them up with a charming wink.
To my manly chest they cling
And their arms around me fling,
Oh dear, what a time I have
When I teach the girls to swim.

My position is one of a deal of trust,
I'm so full of secrets I feel I could bust,
For the way some girls make up's enough to disgust –
Still not a soul I've told
You would be surprised if some girls you could see,

Whose figures you think are from blemish quite free,
Why, do you know – that is – well, between you and me –
Oh! I could a tale unfold.

And then came more patter:

> I could tell you things you'd hardly believe – in fact, I could tell you things
> I don't believe myself. There was a strange lady came to me the other day
> and said, 'Do you mind my swimming with my stockings on?' I said, 'No.'
> Well, out she ran, dived in, and came up feet first – there she was bobbing
> up and down – I didn't know she'd got a cork leg. Another lady asked me
> what I'd charge to teach her to swim. I said, 'One guinea.' She said,
> 'Alright, I shan't be long,' and went into the dressing room, a fine
> strapping figure. When she came out, I didn't know her. I said, 'I'll only
> charge you half a guinea, 'cos there's only half of you to teach.'

The hilarious and cheeky chaps that Dan invented never failed to leave the
audience in stitches, but it was his invention of a dame character
that was to bring him the most fame. It was also this character that began
his career in pantomime. Leno's dame had been spotted by Augustus
Harris, a famous London impresario, when Dan had been working in Drury
Lane. Harris could see the character could be perfectly transported to
the pantomime stage, and so he booked Leno to perform in *Jack and
the Beanstalk*.

Dan's popularity became meteoric through his pantomime appearances,
and he hung up his clogs in favour of high heels and a frock. His quirky
physical appearance, twinkling eyes, cheeky smile and impish expression,
made him the archetypal dame, his role as Mother Goose setting the
benchmark for the part and gaining him much critical acclaim. Now he was
well-paid and never out of a job, managers fell over themselves and their
bank books to engage the finest comic on the London stage. His name was
now known by every man, woman and child in the kingdom, with Queen
Victoria herself numbered amongst his fans. When the 'Old Queen' died in
1901, her son, King Edward VII invited Dan to Sandringham for a command
performance, for which he received a tie-pin and the title 'The King's
Jester'.

By now Dan was suffering from deafness and showing signs of a mental
condition which were indicative of a brain tumour. He would insist at

times that he was descended from a Scottish marquis. Throughout his illness, however, he continued to look out for new routines and influences and he could not fail to be intrigued by the fresh possibilities afforded by moving pictures. In 1902 he and his new stage partner, Herbert Campbell (who had had some success with his comedy act which showed the audience the proper way to eat a new kind of food called spaghetti with hilarious results), made their own film called *Dan Leno and Herbert Campbell Edit The Sun*. It was a short film in which the comedy duo pretended to be newspaper editors working hard in the offices of *The Sun* newspaper. This film footage still exists and is probably the only film of Dan Leno's routines, although it is not a great example of his work; the set and camera work were very crude and it is unlikely that the sketch would have worked on the music-hall stage.

Sadly, soon after his first foray into the world of motion pictures, Dan became critically ill as the brain tumour, which had gradually been stealing his sanity, took the last of his health. When he died aged 43 on 31 October 1904, he had become so famous that every newspaper commemorated his passing. The streets of London were lined with people wishing to bid farewell to their favourite comic as his cortège made its way to Lambeth. His funeral was one of the most highly attended in comedy history.

His life and work became the inspiration for many greats of the comedy stage and screen including Charlie Chaplin, Buster Keaton, George Robey and Stan Laurel. Stan (who we shall come to later in this book), above all others, modelled himself on Dan and adopted some of the facial expressions for which he is best remembered today. Through the work of these great men, Leno's memory lived on.

Postcard of Dan Leno as Widow Twankey

7 BRITANNIA'S FIRST MAKE-OVER

In 1869 John Brand moved on and Britannia Music Hall was to reopen under the new ownership of the Rossboroughs. H.T. Rossborough and his wife were business as well as life partners, with Mrs Rossborough equal in her responsibilities and capabilities. Mr Rossborough had worked for John Brand as the manager of Britannia Music Hall for a number of years, so was well-placed when Brand had decided to sell his interest in the building. Over the decade that Brand had owned the Britannia, he had spent little on maintaining it and the years of smoking, candlelight, coal fires and general wear and tear from the thousands who entered the hall daily had left it thick with grime.

The Rossboroughs were keen to improve the building and began an overhaul which must have cost a considerable amount of money. After several months of closure, the work was completed and Britannia reopened to critical acclaim, the *Glasgow Sentinel*, reporting on 25 September 1869:

> Under Mr. Rossborough's proprietorship the hall has been thoroughly renovated, and can easily now challenge rivalry with any singing-hall in the kingdom. The façade of the building is about the most striking in the city, and for architectural beauty has certainly nothing to rival it. Forming the most imposing building in the Trongate, the Britannia unavoidably deserves the attention of strangers.

The article noted that the performances were playing to packed audiences, representing 'almost every section of the city's population'. Recent adornments to the hall apparently included a pair of much-admired 'elegant lamps, by J&R Fergusson, of Argyle Street'. The doorway and general entrance had been completely remodelled, and three archways 'of Moorish design' led from the entrance to 'a square hall, floored with mosaic, and panelled and painted [by Mr John McKay of Gallowgate] with very great taste indeed'. Two folding doors now led from the hall to the staircases, and these apparently made entering and leaving the auditorium easier and quicker. The roof and other parts of the hall had also been redecorated:

> Boldly panelled and painted in accordance with the mouldings that cross it, the roof of the Britannia, lighted up by many chandeliers, has really a splendid effect. The front of the galleries, the proscenium, the wings of the stage, and all the more prominent points are painted with a due regard to the general effect, and the whole presents a coup d' which must astonish those who are unacquainted with the music halls of Glasgow.

The front gallery now had cushioned seats, attracting 'the better class of visitors' and their families. There was also a series of private boxes at the back of the middle gallery. Dressing rooms had been built over the auditorium; 'stage accessories' had been partially renovated, and the 'scenic decorations' had been replaced, with drop-scenes painted by Mr Fisher.

Decorated column dating from the Rossboroughs' renovation in 1869

Some of this decoration still survives, notably the star-spangled night sky, which today peeks through later layers of thick paint, and a sumptuously decorated column which is hidden behind a later addition to the building.

The article is not just complimentary to the Rossboroughs' taste in design, but concludes with a word about Mr Rossborough himself: 'Indeed, few public men can lay claim to the place Mr Rossborough holds in the estimation of the public, and under his proprietorship, the Britannia is fated to continue the wonderfully popular career.'

All of this positive publicity had reached the ears of Mr Baylis, owner of the Scotia Music Hall on Stockwell Street. Not wanting to be out-done by his Trongate neighbours, he sought out the tradesman who had upholstered the Britannia's seats. When he asked the upholsterer if he could 'do the same for the Scotia' the upholsterer asked, 'What do you want the seats covered with?' To which Mr Baylis reportedly replied, 'Arses at 2d each.'

The Rossboroughs had certainly put their stamp on the place, but they didn't stop there. They had spent a considerable amount of money on upgrading the hall and they certainly weren't going to let it get fouled up by men coming in straight from their work places covered in filth. Clean clothes and a tidy appearance were insisted upon 'with very considerable advantage to the workmen', who were not allowed in unless they paid attention to their cleanliness. Rossborough led the way with this. His attempt to smarten up the audience was further commented upon in December 1869 when a review of his entertainments in the Glasgow Sentinel also included the following statement: 'Britannia is the place of amusement in which the working man may spend the evening with advantage to his pocket, the cultivation of his musical taste and to the improvement of his manners.' A very unusual boast indeed for a music hall, and, as it transpires, a very short-lived one.

8 THE RISE OF BURLESQUE

By this time novelty acts and burlesque had become popular and were far removed from the basic fare the turns that the Free and Easies had offered. This new breed of act demanded slightly more lavish surroundings. Suddenly music hall became more vibrant.

The origin of burlesque performance is generally attributed to Aristophanes, the Greek writer who nearly 2,500 years ago wrote the first political satires and comic dramas in which he parodied well-known figures. His plays were hugely popular and were performed all over Greece. In his lifetime Aristophanes's humorous take on politics and famous people and incidents caused a fair bit of controversy, particularly his comments on Athens, which resulted in him being prosecuted several times. A generation later Plato featured Aristophanes as a character in his Symposium, in which he gave a comical account of the origin of love.

The origin of the word 'burlesque' itself is thought to derive from one of several sources. In sixteenth-century Italy, a bored young clerk called Francesco Berni began writing comical poems to entertain himself and his friends. His clever and witty verses quickly gained him notoriety, in certain literary circles, as a great humorist. Berni used the term 'burlesque' (literally meaning mockery) to describe his work. His talent for making others laugh at the world belied the realities of his own life, which was, to say the least, a bit odd.

He spent most of his life living in Rome and working within the Vatican walls as a secretary to the secretary of the pope. He was a devoutly religious man at a time when the cries for religious reformation were rumbling across Europe and threatening to usurp the Catholic monopoly on Christianity. Berni appears to have supported the push for reformation, although evidently not enough to abandon his church, as in 1530 he obtained a canonry from Florence Cathedral.

The Vatican was not without scandal and Berni found himself living in a world where piety constantly fought alongside corruption as the Italian nobility had a great deal of influence within the Vatican. Berni himself did the best he could to avoid being dragged through the mire of Italian society, but sadly this refusal to participate in the corrupt activities of his colleagues and the aristocracy resulted in his early demise, when, in 1536, he was poisoned by the Duke Alessandro de Medici, apparently because Berni had refused to poison the duke's cousin.

Berni's legacy was a collection of sparklingly witty work, so popular that burlesque poems became referred to as *poesie bernesca*.

The other possible origin of the word can be traced directly back to the Commedia dell' Arte where, for comic effect, the principal characters would slap the other players with a padded stick called a 'burle'.

In Britain, burlesque dates back to the seventeenth century, a time when it had become a popular practice to ridicule famous literary works and lampoon the dramatic styles of the time, which generally took themselves far too seriously. Examples of early English burlesque usually cited are *The Rehearsal*, by Buckingham (1671), *The Beggars' Opera*, by John Gay (1728) which satirised the traditional conventions of opera, and *The Critic*, by Sheridan (1779), which parodied the heroic dramas of the time.

By the end of the eighteenth century, this burlesquing often included a lot of sexual innuendo and bawdy humour, a trait which was to remain a common thread throughout music-hall burlesque history.

In the nineteenth century, British burlesque moved away from its literary roots and began to parody everyday life. Burlesque performance also started to include a more musical thread known as burletta, which was very popular indeed in halls like Britannia, particularly in the early days when the management couldn't afford the licence fees paid on the more extravagant dramatic productions of the larger patented theatres. The burlettas were musical farces that depicted events and characters, using humour, dance, music and physical comedy. Some of the early burlettas still found their origins in classical drama, but had added comedy songs, exaggerated characters and slapstick routines. The popularity of burletta, in fact, continued into the early years of the twentieth century: in January of 1901, it made a well-received return to Britannia, the playbill advertising 'Angeloti, The Celebrated Hungarian Protean Artiste' in 'a unique instrumental, vocal and character play' entitled *Thompson's Five Guinea Clients*, in which Angeloti played all the characters.

Women were an essential part of nineteeth-century burlesque and their performances and success on the music-hall stage had a small part to play in the battle for women's independence. For the first time, the ladies of the music hall had an opportunity to be saucy and provocative and two of the ladies who took full advantage of the naughty genre were Miss Marie Lloyd and Miss Marie Loftus, two of the most remarkable divas of the music-hall burlesque stage.

⑨ MR AND MRS ROSSBOROUGH
PROUDLY PRESENT

MARIE LLOYD: THE QUEEN
OF THE MUSIC HALL

Born Matilda Victoria Wood in 1870, Marie Lloyd is still remembered today as one of the brightest burlesque stars of the music hall. Although there is no documentary evidence to prove it, it is extremely likely that she performed at the Britannia in the early part of her career, and no history of music-hall entertainment is complete without a mention of her extraordinary life.

The eldest of nine children, Marie grew up in Hoxton, London. Her father was a gentle soul who made artificial flowers during the day and worked as a waiter in the Royal Eagle tavern by night. Marie's mother also worked hard, as a dressmaker, a skill of which her daughters would take full advantage in future years.

From childhood, Marie and her sisters had all aspired to becoming big stars of the stage. Helped by their mother, they made colourful costumes and wrote comical sketches and ditties based on the popular minstrel acts. They called their little troupe The Fairy Bells and performed in some of the local church and Temperance halls. Marie's sisters, Rosie, Alice and Daisy, all had a certain amount of success as adults on the professional stage and all starred as principal boys in pantomimes, but Marie was the only one to truly

Postcard of Marie Lloyd

achieve her ambition to be one of the greatest performers the music hall had ever known.

Marie began her stage career as an amateur act at the Grecian. At first she adopted the stage name Bella Delamare and performed a couple of songs before ending with a rousing Irish jig, which Marie herself confessed received thunderous applause from her first music-hall audiences. Her amateur act did not go unnoticed and she was given a week's contract to perform at Belmont's Sebright Hall in Hackney Road. Her first week's engagement earned her the princely sum of 5 shillings and led to bookings in three halls every night. Before long she found herself racing across London to fulfil her various contracts.

The name Bella Delamare was only just becoming known about town when she suddenly decided to change it to the simpler, somewhat less tarty, Marie Lloyd. In one of her acts, she dressed in the innocent, crisp pinafore of a schoolgirl and sang her own version of the popular song 'The Boy I Love is up in the Gallery'.

By the age of 17, Marie was already earning good money and was chased by dozens of adoring fans, who lingered hopefully around the stage door each night. Marie's heart, however, had already been won by the man she was to marry, Percy Courtenay. Actually, and rather scandalously for the time, Percy was to be the first of three husbands. Poor Marie seems to have had a great gift for choosing the wrong man. Percy was a tout at the local racetrack – not exactly a regular or well-paid occupation. It must have been hard for a man at that time to live in the shadow of his wife's fame and fortune and, before too long, he began to drink. Unfortunately, when drunk, he often launched violent attacks on Marie.

Together they had a daughter, and for the sake of that child and her own reputation, Marie endured her marriage for six years before taking the brave step of leaving Percy in 1893. In 1894, she was granted a separation on the grounds that she feared for the lives of her daughter and herself.

As her marriage disintegrated, her career bloomed. She had become famous for her saucy routines, where she would wink and gesture suggestively at the audience, changing the meaning of the most innocent song or taking advantage of more provocative verses, like those of 'Every Little Movement', always a favourite number. She would glide elegantly onto the stage wearing an enormous chapeau and an elegant, jewel-encrusted, figure-enhancing gown which cinched her waist and exaggerated her voluptuous bosom. A split up the front of her skirt exposed a considerable length of shapely leg. As she sang she would emphasise the meaning of the verses with winks and wiggles.

Up to the West End, right in the Best End,
Straight from the country came Miss Maudie Brown.
Father's a curate, but couldn't endure it,
That's why the Lady is residing in town.
Twelve months ago her modest self felt quite sublime
To sit on a fellow's knee who's been all in the grime!
And if you should want a kiss,
She'd drop her eyes like this,
But now she drops them just one at a time.

And every little movement has a meaning of its own,
Every little movement tells a tale.
When she walks in dainty hobbles,
At the back round here, there's a kind of wibble-wobble;
And she glides like this,
Then the Johnnies follow in her trail,
'Cos when she turns her head like so,
Something's going, don't you know,
Every little movement tells a tale.

Down by the blue sea, cute as she could be,
Maudie would go for her dip every day.
Maudie has an eye for the boys, Oh my!
And it happens that Reggie was passing that way.
When Reggie saw her he fell into a trance,
He too is going bathing for her now, here's a chance.
She didn't smile or frown,
Just threw her signal down!
Then slyly shrugged her shoulders with a glance.

And every little movement has a meaning of its own,
Every little movement tells a tale.
When she dashed into the ocean,
Reggie kept close by for to know her
Maudie tried to swim:
'Oh I'm here,' said Reggie, 'if you fail,'

And in less than half a wink,
Maudie dear commenced to sink,
Every little movement tells a tale.

Congratulations, such celebrations,
Bertie and Gertie have just tied the knot.
Both at the party, all gay and hearty,
And noticed the bridegroom looks anxious, eh what?
When friends and relatives depart their different ways,
Alone with the girlie of his heart.
And once again he turned the lights down low,
She looked at him like so,
Then shyly with her wedding ring she played.

And every little movement has a meaning of its own,
Every little movement tells a tale.
When alone no words they utter,
But when midnight chimed, then their hearts begin to flutter.
And she yawned like this,
And stretches out her arm so frail,
And her hubby full of love,
Looks at her and points above,
Every little movement tells a tale.

Her act was regarded as so close to the bone that Marie found herself up in front of the Vigilance Committee after a complaint from Mrs Ormiston Chant of the Purity Party. Mrs Chant had been most offended by Miss Lloyd's lewd behaviour on the stage of the London Empire. Marie easily survived the scrutiny of the committee by singing one of her songs without her customary winks and gestures and presenting a demeanour most convincingly innocent. She then sang 'Come into the Garden, Maud' and added every saucy trick she knew until the song appeared the raunchiest number ever written. Somehow this demonstration got past the committee and after she promised that she would be a good girl, she was allowed to continue her life as a music-hall star.

She did not, however, clean up her act. Her saucy implications were what had made her one of the most popular acts on the stage and she was damned if she was going to lose them, even when her closest friends warned her that at times her act was positively indecent.

In 1896 Marie packed her bags and departed for South Africa, where she embarked on a highly successful tour which included her daughter on the billing as 'Little Maudie Courtenay', and was the debut of what would become one of Marie's most popular songs, 'Oh! Mr Porter':

Lately I just spent a week with my old Aunt Brown,
Came up to see wond'rous sights of famous London Town.
Just a week I had of it, all round the place we'd roam
Wasn't I sorry on the day I had to go back home?
Worried about with packing, I arrived late at the station,
Dropped my hatbox in the mud, the things all fell about,
Got my ticket, said 'good-bye', 'Right away,' the guard did cry,
But I found the train was wrong and shouted out:

Chorus:
Oh! Mr Porter, what shall I do?
I want to go to Birmingham
And they're taking me on to Crewe,
Send me back to London as quickly as you can,
Oh! Mr Porter, what a silly girl I am!

The porter would not stop the train, but I laughed and said, 'You must
Keep your hair on, Mary Ann, and mind that you don't bust.'
Some old gentleman inside declared that it was hard,
Said, 'Look out of the window, Miss, and try and call the guard.'
Didn't I, too, with all my might I nearly balanced over,
But my old friend grasp'd my leg, and pulled me back again,
Nearly fainting with the fright, I sank into his arms a sight,
Went into hysterics but I cried in vain:

Chorus repeats

On his clean old shirt-front then I laid my trembling head,
'Do take it easy, rest awhile,' the dear old chappie said.
If you make a fuss of me and on me do not frown,
You shall have my mansion, dear, away in London Town.
Wouldn't you think me silly if I said I could not like him?
Really he seemed a nice old boy, so I replied this way;

'I will be your own for life, your imay doodle um little wife,
If you'll never tease me any more I say.'

Chorus repeats

In 1897 and hot on the heels of her success in Africa, Marie and her daughter travelled to America, where she discovered her reputation as a saucy songstress had preceded her. Concerned conservative members of the public picketed the theatres where Marie was billed and prevented the audiences from entering. In the *New York Telegraph* Marie defended her name by declaring that her audiences at home did not pay good money to hear the Salvation Army: 'If I was to try to sing highly moral songs they would fire beer bottles and beer mugs at me. I can't help it if people want to turn and twist my meanings.' The moral outcry and resulting press coverage ensured that her tour of America was a sell-out, and whilst some of the more cautious managers were terrified that Marie might live up to her reputation, the audience earnestly hoped that she did.

On her return to Britain, she continued to pack the halls. Soon after returning to London, she met and fell in love Alec Hurley, a singer. At this time her divorce from Percy was still not final, so for many years the couple lived together outside of marriage. To avoid scandal they travelled to Australia where Marie's private affairs had not been quite as publicly discussed. After only a few months, though, they came back to Britain, keeping their private affair as private as they possibly could until Marie's divorce was finally granted in 1905. In 1906 wedding bells finally rang for a second time. Alec doted on Marie and she doted on him, that is, until she met Bernard Dillon, a promising young jockey who was nearly half her age. In 1910 she left Alec to live with Bernard, who, though much younger than Marie, was obviously besotted with the woman who was now known as 'The Queen of the Music Hall'.

Bernard's adoration did not survive long into their relationship, however, which slowly became a repeat of her first marriage: he lost his licence as a jockey, and, with his career finished, he tried a new pursuit as a drunk. Marie, however, stuck by him.

In the shadow of her scandalous private life, Marie's stage fortunes had also begun to change. Although her name was still one of the biggest crowd-pullers, her reputation for lewd burlesquing and seducing young men saw her name left off the programme for the first Royal Music Hall

Command Performance in 1912. Feeling slighted by this omission, Marie opened her own show on the same night in the London Pavilion with the heading 'Every Performance by Marie Lloyd is a Command Performance by Order of the British Public'. Her show was, as always, a phenomenal success, but Marie had been deeply wounded at not being invited to the Royal Command Performance when all of her fellow music-hall stars had been included in the programme.

Still stinging from the slight, Marie decided to try America again. She and Bernard took a passage together, travelling under the name Mr and Mrs Dillon. Of course they weren't really married – she was still Mrs Hurley, a fact that was detected when she failed to provide the American authorities with proof of her identity as Mrs Dillon. With the scandalous nature of their relationship uncovered, the couple were arrested for 'moral turpitude' and sent to Ellis Island until a passage back to England could be secured. Their prison sentence lasted a full week before two berths were found on the *Olympic*, but as the couple were about to board, word came that Marie could continue her tour of America if she paid bail of £300 and did not share accommodation with her travelling companion. She paid the bail and assured the authorities that she and Bernard would live separately, which they did for the following weeks as Marie began her second American tour. Then Marie received the tragic news that her real husband, Alec Hurley, had died quite suddenly. By the time the news reached her, he had already been buried, and when she returned to Britain a few weeks later, she was legally Mrs Bernard Dillon.

When the First World War broke out, Marie did her bit to help enlist soldiers, visit hospitals and keep up the spirits of the British public. By the end of the war, though, Marie was beginning to suffer. Bernard had now started to become a violent drunk, driving Marie to start drinking excessively herself. Finally, after Bernard had attacked Marie's elderly father, the couple parted ways and Marie lived out the remaining few years of her life as a single woman. She still performed nightly, but now her voice was becoming weak and corrupted by alcohol abuse. In October 1922 she staggered onto the stage and sang 'It's a Bit of a Ruin that Cromwell Knocked About a Bit':

> *In the gay old days there used to be something doing,*
> *No wonder that the poor old abbey went to ruin.*
> *Those who raise their voices sing and shout of it,*

You can bet your life there isn't a doubt of it.
Outside the Oliver Cromwell last Saturday night
I was one of the ruins that Cromwell knocked about a bit.

At the end she collapsed, and everyone applauded in the belief that she had just been acting the drunk. However, her collapse was a result of physical and emotional stress, and she died just three days later, a tragic end for the Queen of the Music Hall.

MARIE LOFTUS: THE SARAH BERNHARDT
OF THE MUSIC HALL

Marie Loftus is more famous today for being the mother of Cissie (Celia) Loftus who was one of the greatest stars of the stage, her abilities spanning classical theatre and music, as well as music hall. Marie Loftus herself had also been a great star in her day and until recently there has been little written about the great lady.

Marie Loftus was born in 1857 in Glasgow, only a stone's throw away from Britannia, in Stockwell Street. Her early life was spent as a juvenile performer on the stages of the Glasgow music halls where she performed with another girl, but it was her solo act that was to gain her acclaim.

Marie began her solo career singing the Irish ballads that were popular in the Glasgow halls. They were a safe routine in Scotland, but when she was invited to perform in London, she soon discovered the audience preferred a less sentimental routine and as her London appearances became more frequent, she changed her act to suit the city's crowd, adding a little more burlesque to her routine. She became an expert at parodying the other popular turns of the day. Her ability as an actress meant she could happily mimic a wide range of styles, from opera divas to fellow music-hall starlets, but her talent as a singer would see her billed alongside such idols as Dan Leno and Marie Lloyd.

Loftus found her greatest success when she donned a pinafore and played the schoolgirl, as naughty as she was sweet. She could be coy, saucy or coquettish as the number demanded, her shapely figure, handsome features and abundant sex appeal gaining the admiration of a generation of men who likened her to the greatest female sex symbol the stage had ever known, Sarah Bernhardt.

Postcard of Marie Loftus

No matter how successful Marie was in London and around the provinces, she always loved going home to Glasgow, where she was nicknamed the 'Hibernian Hebe' and was welcomed with a heartiness rarely seen outside of that city. When she returned to Britannia in 1894, the little hall was packed from ceiling to floor and she was, according to the *Evening Times*, 'cheered to the echo'. Her success prompted the then proprietor, William Kean, to double the admission price; still thousands queued to see her, and those that didn't manage to get in hung around the Trongate, waiting for a glimpse of their heroine. The resultant gathering blocked the street of traffic and police had to be called to disperse the crowd. The public was further enchanted by her when she ordered 150 pairs of shoes to be distributed amongst the poor children of the East End.

Marie's success continued into the twentieth century, but by now her own daughter, Celia, who had started as Marie's dresser, was making a meteoric rise which would eclipse her mother's fame. In 1912 both Marie and Celia appeared on the bill at the Royal Music Hall Command Performance. This was one of the last appearances Marie would make on the London stage. By the time she died in 1940, her name had long since been forgotten, except by those few who saw and fell in love with her.

Her songs are not as well remembered today as those of some of her contemporaries. They include: 'Sister Mary Wants to Know', 'I'm so Shy', 'She Lisped When She Said Yes' and 'Girls, We Would Never Stand It': *'When first they come courting, how nice they behave, / For a smile or a kiss, how humbly they crave / But when once a girl's wed, she's a drudge and a slave / . . . I think we would all prefer marriage with strife, / Than be on the shelf and nobody's wife.'*

Marie Loftus may have been famous for her wicked delivery and female allure, but ironically the British burlesque of the music-hall stages did not feature a continuous parade of feminine and exotic divas in glamorous gowns or saucy schoolgirl garb. There were, in fact, many female performers who dressed as men. This cross-dressing gave the ladies an opportunity to sing bawdier, more boisterous numbers and Britannia was fortunate enough to be graced by many male impersonators, including the most famous of them all, Miss Vesta Tilley.

MISS VESTA TILLEY

Vesta was born in Worcester in 1864. She was christened Matilda Alice Powles, but was generally called Tilley, an abbreviation of Matilda. At the age of three she began working on the professional stage. Her father, Henry Powles, had until the late 1850s been a factory worker, but lured by the bright lights of the world of theatre, had devised a short act and embarked upon a life in the music halls. His act (of which there is little record) seems, however, to have been less than popular with the audiences, so instead, Henry cultivated his talent as a chairman and adopted the stage name Harry Ball. In 1867 he was employed as the chairman in the Theatre Royal in Gloucester.

By this time his daughter was only three years old, but surrounded by theatrical types, she was already showing a gift for entertaining. She loved being the centre of attention and would endeavour to amuse her family with her little dance routines, inspiring her father to put her on the bill at the Royal and to try her in front of a real audience. It seems that little Tilley was an instant hit.

In 1868 Harry became the chairman at the St George's Music Hall in Nottingham, and he took 'The Great Little Tilley' (as she was now billed) with him. Before long, the little girl was capturing the hearts of all who saw her and other music halls were interested in engaging her. She travelled to Leicester, Dudley and Derby, usually escorted by her father, who doted on his little girl. Then, one day, he went into the dressing room to see if she was ready to go on stage, and he caught her trying on his coat. She paced the dressing room in a comical take-off of her father. He promptly bought a bolt of fabric, which he gave to his wife Matilda, who used her dressmaking skills to create a miniature suit in the fashionable mode of the time. In 1870, dressed in her own little top-hat and tails, Tilley sang some of the songs made popular by the tenor Sim Reeves, founding the act which was to make her famous.

The young girl's role as the upper-class fop was incredibly comical. She would swagger across the stage singing songs such as 'Burlington Bertie', 'The Eton Boys' and 'The Gaiety Boys', which had been made popular by other leading stars of the day. Her male impersonations were an instant success and before long she was receiving £5 per week for her appearances.

By the age of 10 she was offered a tour of the London halls, and within months was heralded as 'The London Idol'. It was during the London tours that she changed her name to Vesta, as she was now beginning to grow out of the title

Postcard of Vesta Tilley

'The Great Little Tilley'. Vesta was the Roman goddess of fire, and was also the name of a very popular brand of matches; it was therefore easy for the audience to remember. At the time, it was a name unique to her as a performer, but over the years, as her fame grew, the name was adopted by other ladies of the halls.

By now Vesta was performing up to seven shows a night and her father was forced to employ a manager to look after his daughter's business affairs, leaving him to concentrate on his own career and help his wife with their ever-growing family (he and Matilda had 13 children in all).

In 1877, aged 13, Vesta performed in her first pantomime, in Portsmouth, taking on the role of principle boy. She was to set the benchmark for principle boys, and her easy presence and skill at portraying the male romantic or heroic lead ensured that pantomime would become a regular feature in her annual diary. She loved pantomime, her favourite role being that of Dick Whittington, although she also played Sinbad the Sailor and the prince in *Sleeping Beauty*. However, Dick was a role she was to reprise again and again over her career. Demand for Vesta in pantomime was so strong that she found herself being booked years in advance, and was even offered a pantomime scheduled at Easter to please her public.

Even at the height of her success her appearances in pantomime charmed not only the audiences but her fellow cast members as well. She had a great affection for the children she performed with, her early start on the stage perhaps provoking in her a unique understanding of the long hours the juveniles worked. She loved to give the younger stars special treats as the following report in *Barr's Professional Gazette* (February 1893) illustrates:

> On Monday afternoon, 20 February, Miss Vesta Tilley, who as Dick Whittington in the Royal Pantomime has won such favour from those in front and on the stage, entertained the 45 children employed in the pantomime to tea in the wardrobe rooms of the theatre . . . What with all the good things, crackers, 'blindman's buff,' and other children's games, the pretty little maidens were still able to play as well as ever their various parts in the evening.

The 1880s saw Vesta venture north of the border and into Scotland where, in the first week of August 1885, the Britannia audience was treated to 'The Male Impersonations of Vesta Tilley'. Her name was not so well known in Glasgow and was listed near the bottom of a bill which included such greats as Monsieur Carl Halay, 'the monarch of all gymnasts', the Murphys with their 'excellent Hibernian entertainments' and Mr. W.H. Vane's 'clever banjo manipulation'. The audience had been in a good mood that week, which was the first under the new management of Mr A. McGowan and his personal secretary Tom McClymont. Britannia was now proclaimed 'the best and pre-eminently most popular place of amusement in Glasgow' and Vesta won over the most discerning audience in town with effortless ease. Amongst her list of popular tunes she sang what would become one of her most famous, 'I'm Following in Father's Footsteps':

To follow in your father's footsteps,
Is a motto for each boy.
And following in father's footsteps,
Is a thing I much enjoy.
My mother caught me out, one evening
Up the West End, on the spree;
She said, 'Where are you going?'
But I answered, 'Don't ask me!'

'I'm following in father's footsteps,
I'm following me dear old dad
He's just in front with a fine big gal,
So I thought that I'd have one as well.
I don't know where he's going,
But when he gets there I'll be glad!
I'm following in father's footsteps, Yes,
I'm following me dear old dad!'

Pa said that to the north of England
He on business had to go;
To Charing Cross he went,
And there he booked,
I booked first class also.
I found myself, that night, in Paris!
To the clergyman, next door,
I answered, when he said,
'What are you in this gay place for?'

'I'm following in father's footsteps,
I'm following me dear old dad.
He's travelling now for his firm, you see,
In fancy goods, it seems to me.
I don't know where he's going,
But when he gets there I'll be glad!
I'm following in father's footsteps, Yes,
I'm following me dear old dad!'

The song goes on, with the narrator following his father around Britain on more dubious escapades.

Vesta Tilley's week-long engagement gave the audience a taste for male impersonators and over the following years many others followed in her cross-dressing footsteps: Miss Carrie Bernhardt; Miss Amy Victor; Miss Nellie May and Miss Katie Lawrence (the original *Daisy Bell*) to name but a few.

In 1889 her father died. He had been not just her father and manager, but also her dearest friend and trusted confidant, and his death saddened her deeply. Vesta leaned upon her friend Walter de Frece, a music-hall owner in

London. Their relationship bloomed and in 1890 they were married in Brixton. Like her father had been, de Frece remained throughout their life together a constant support to Vesta, and she likewise to him.

Vesta was popular with all audiences: men appreciated her for her songs and comical send-ups of their sex, whilst women idolised her for her parodies of males and their foibles. Her characters included, amongst others, a sailor, a soldier, a fop, a policeman and a bell hop. In 1912, her talent received attention from the royal household and she was asked to perform at the first Royal Music Hall Command Performance. The character she chose was 'Piccadilly Johnny with the Little Glass Eye', who was introduced as 'the most perfectly dressed young man in the house'.

By now Vesta was a veteran of the music halls and the burlesque tradition, and, although not the originator of the male impersonator routine, she kept this style of performance popular in theatres across the world, counting America in her list of conquests.

In the First World War, Vesta did her part as a soldier – not on the front-line of the battle fields, but on the front-line of her husband's music halls. She would dress in uniform and sing what would become the most famous songs of her career, 'The Army of Today's Alright', 'Jolly Good Luck to the Girl who Loves a Soldier' and 'I've Got a Bit of a Blighty One': '*When I think about my dugout, where I dare not stick my mug out . . . / I'm glad I've got a bit of a blighty one.*'

This last song was regarded as rather controversial in certain quarters, as it told the tale of a soldier who was basically fed up with the horrors of war and wanted to go home, no matter how bad an injury he had to incur in the process – not a popular sentiment when the government was working hard trying to enlist men to fight for king and country. 'A blighty one' was the nickname given by soldiers to an injury which was severe enough to result in them being taken out of the war and sent back home to dear old Blighty.

The content of the song, however, did little to put off prospective conscripts, who loved Vesta's portrayal of 'The Tommy in the Trench' and 'Jack Tar Home from Sea'. At the height of the war, Vesta performed for the servicemen in hospital and sold war bonds, whilst de Frece carried on trying to enlist fresh soldiers from the audiences in his music halls. De Frece's endeavours did not go unrecognised, and in 1919 he received a knighthood. The new title signalled the end of Vesta's stage career – soon after Walter's knighthood, she hung up her breeches and donned a dress:

perhaps male impersonation and performance didn't seem appropriate anymore, or perhaps she just felt that it was time to retire in order to concentrate on her new role as Lady de Frece.

In 1935, Walter died in Monte Carlo, where the couple had been living for several years. With her husband gone, Vesta moved back to Britain and settled in the seaside resort of Hove where she lived out the rest of her retirement as a comfortably wealthy lady. Her retirement lasted a well-deserved 32 years – she had, after all, worked since she was three – and she died in 1952, aged 88. Her ashes are buried beneath a lilac tree in Golders Green crematorium, London.

OOH LA LA!

Today, people generally think of burlesque as far more iniquitous than women dressing as men and swaggering around parodying male foibles, or grown women dressed up as schoolgirls. The general expectation for a burlesque show today consists of women prancing across the stage and taunting the viewer with naughty flashes of flesh, and this sort of entertainment has been a staple of the music hall since its beginnings.

The classic melody 'Ta-Ra-Ra-Boum-De-Ay' is evocative in its very name of the brasher, bawdier fare on offer. This particular song was a familiar tune in the music halls and singing saloons the length and breadth of Britain, and it translated happily across Europe and even into West Africa, where, according to *Barr's Professional Gazette*, it was received with some enthusiasm:

Boys clad simply in their shirts, and men with no shirts, but only coats and trousers, occupied the reserved seats. One of the singers gave Ta-ra-ra-boum-de-ay with the usual gymnastic accompaniments. This had a magic affect. The shirtless gentlemen of the reserved seats, and those attired in simply that garment, rose as one man, and under the spirited air of Ta-ra-ra shot up their legs and sent forth their boum-de-ays. The timid portion of the audience retired, and the whole place was given up to the devotees of Ta-ra-ra. The seats offered no impediment to the perfect performance of the dance, and the yells of the hackneyed song sounded throughout the whole building, and any further attempt to proceed with the concert was prevented for that evening.

The can-can was another routine to set the heart racing. Although traditionally associated with the music halls of Paris, such as the Moulin Rouge and the Folies Bergère, it was performed in halls all over the world. In Britannia Music Hall it was performed several times during the 1870s and 1890s as a climax to the evening's entertainments. During one performance, five girls ran on stage wearing tight bodices that revealed ample cleavage, their tiny corseted waists supporting the heavy skirts which were weighed down with brass sequins, embroidery and beads. As the orchestra played they became a whirling flurry of colour as layer upon layer of frilly petticoats were lifted to show off what the girls wore beneath. (In some less reputable houses the girls showed what they *didn't* wear beneath. Britannia, however, was a clean, family establishment and knickerbockers were a requirement.)

Combined with gymnastic cartwheels, splits, and the whoops and shouts of the dancers as the music rose to a frenzied crescendo, the can-can was a merry jig that could not fail to raise the spirits, but it was just one of the burlesque dances that the Britannia audience enjoyed. High-kicking competitions, where dancing girls lifted their skirts and kicked their legs high to impress the audience, were incredibly popular and appeared on the bill far more often than the can-can.

Dancer's skirt now on display in the auditorium

The music hall in the 1870s, with its risqué burlesque, battled against the sensitivities of the moral population of Glasgow and great concern was expressed.

An article in the *North British Daily Mail* (February 1875) of the time tells of Mr John Burns, a moral champion, who invited a collection of Glasgow worthies to attend a meeting in the Religious Institution Rooms in order to establish whether the content of these shows should be of enough concern as to warrant the attention of the magistrates and the lord provost. The meeting was called on 25 February 1875 and 'there was a very crowded attendance of the most influential citizens of Glasgow'.

During this meeting, gentlemen who had been asked to visit several halls were asked to relate their experiences of the singing saloons and describe what they had seen. Some of the details were, they said, so shocking that they would not state them in words, unless it became absolutely necessary for the purposes of the investigation. The gentlemen did, however, offer the following description:

> Young women, so scantily clothed as to be almost naked, danced upon stages before crowds of men sitting drinking beer and spirits, and smoking cigars and pipes; whilst men sang songs both blasphemous and filthy, containing, as they did, suggestions of a coarse and indecent nature. There were, however, parts of the entertainment which were not only quite unobjectionable, but very good; but should a visitor stay an entire evening, he could scarcely fail to hear and see what was highly improper.

The article then went on to describe young men who 'had gone astray – not through the influence of drink, but from their frequently attending such so-called places of entertainment'. The time had come, it seemed, for magistrates to 'exercise a particular surveillance in this direction'. The meeting concluded, with all attending in agreement that the provost and magistrates should be contacted with their concerns so that some action could be taken.

On 1 March 1875, a meeting with over 200 attendees was held in the police court hall. Lord Provost Bain occupied the bench with eight bailies of the city, the police clerk and the chief constable. Things were getting very serious.

Mr John Burns made his address:

. . . it cannot be denied that outwardly respectable people are among the frequenters of those places of amusement, where they are mostly entertained with the abominable . . . the young men of our city have been in the habit of visiting these saloons, where every evil influence is at work to break down their self-respect and ruin them morally and physically . . . more young men have gone wrong by the instrumentality of singing saloons than from any other cause in this city . . . it is inconceivable that anything more degrading or licentious could be witnessed in a place where neither Christianity nor civilisation had ever entered, far less in a city where religion and philanthropy abound . . . It is quite possible that one may spend an hour or two in one or other of these places without finding any cause of complaint; but when you have a full report of an entire evening's entertainment, it is to a greater or less extent of all, that during some part or other of the evening, songs are sung and words are spoken and dances are danced which are either wholly or partially indecent. Frequently it is by gestures or interjected words and sentiments that this is made apparent; but at other times both words and actions are so grossly indecent that they will not bear public relation. It is in the spoken parts that the chief opportunities are taken for profanity and lewdness.

Certainly it seems that in Britannia, at least, the moral content of the performances was considered in light of this meeting and the concern in the press, and the assertion 'The management would like to state that the performance is not meant to offend . . .' then appeared on a notice in the foyer.

THE BLACK FACE OF BRITANNIA

Not all the entertainments presented on the music-hall stage, however, were regarded as morally suspect. Minstrels were another immensely popular act and their performances were widely accepted as good, honest, family fun. Traditionally, white people would 'black up' using burnt cork and boot-black in order to perform parodies of black people. In some troupes, black people also blacked up to participate in a lampoon of themselves. Although today we may regard this form of entertainment as xenophobic, in the British music halls of the nineteenth century, it was enjoyed innocently enough, the majority of people at the time merely seeing it as a highly amusing act, not as a political or racist comment.

The act originated in the 1830s in America, where it was based on the tragedy of slavery and minstrel troupes became ubiquitous on the music-hall stages of Britain from the 1860s. Although the performers would dance, sing and clown around, they also infused the sketches with the pathos of plantation life and the act served perhaps to promote a little bit more understanding of the hardships these people had suffered.

In Britannia minstrels were a regular and extremely popular addition to the bill. In 1869 an advertisement for the Britannia extols the virtues of 'The Cedas Minstrels' who 'in conjunction with Messrs Cobb and East, supplied the African element so necessary for every musical evening'.

The minstrel troupes themselves were large enough to account for half of the evening's entertainment. Through songs, sketches and comic routines the performers would portray black people in both negative and positive ways, as lazy, idiotic, ignorant, quick-witted or joyous. These shows were often highlighted by 'stump speeches' which poked fun at all sorts of subjects, and were punctuated by the use of an exaggerated imitation of the African American vernacular for comical affect. For example, the performer might begin by addressing the audience with, 'Belubed brudders and brudderesses, I hab been requested to come down here dis ebening to gib you my opinion on some things that hab neber happened to me, nor anyone here, dere or yonder . . .'

The sketches often touched upon the more serious side of black history and were generally billed as the event of the evening. One such sketch, 'The White Slave, or Life in Old Kentucky' was presented in eight scenes and was a prominent feature on the Britannia bill in February 1895. It was

Signed postcard of
Florence Yaymen,
a female black-
faced performer

quickly followed by the engagement of Mr Will Candish, 'Negro comedian', who in contrast to the thought-provoking 'Life in Old Kentucky', presented a hilarious rendition of 'Dorothy Dean' on the bagpipes.

In Britannia, it seems that black-faced entertainers were so popular that all sorts of performers began to emulate aspects of the act; take for example another Britannia favourite, 'The Unique Sam Jackson, negro comedian, banjoist and Hungarian top-boot dancer'.

Some of the names used by the minstrels to describe their characters are certainly not regarded as politically correct today. Many of them, in fact, are regarded as being highly offensive and far more obscene than a flash of a can-can girl's gusset. One of the most famous minstrel performers of them all, G.H. Elliot, was often billed as 'the Chocolate-Coloured Coon' and the terms 'kaffir', 'negro' and 'nigger' were also used with great frequency.

Until the end of the nineteenth century, the minstrel troupes comprised of only male performers; women didn't perform in these acts until the 1890s, when they began to appear on a regular basis as part of the troupe. In November 1896, 'Four Daisies and the Coon – vocalists, speciality dancers and high-kickers' appeared at the Britannia: four girls in colourful dresses kicked their legs in the tradition of the can-can as an accompaniment to the blacked-up male singer.

At this time in Glasgow, the only black face to be seen in the audience was probably that of an unwashed coal miner. As life was generally a struggle for the working classes, beset by oppressions and difficulties, the minstrel shows contained much that the audience could identify with.

By the 1920s, in America, political campaigning saw the negative racist portrayals of the blacked-up performer go out of favour, and vaudeville took its place on the stage. In Britain, however, minstrel shows remained popular, and even in the age of television they were a regular feature of variety shows until the 1970s. Amateur minstrel groups occasionally appeared in community theatres until the late 1980s, but in recent years of increased cultural understanding, the outdated racial stereotype has disappeared.

THE LIONS COMIQUES

George Leybourne and the Great Vance were the two first recognised heart-throbs of the music hall. They were also rivals. Their handsome good looks, rakish charm and immaculate deportment made them the suavest of comics as they burlesqued upper-class swells. Their swaggering depictions of champagne-soaked louts attracted a large audience wherever they went and their larger-than-life stage personas and whiskers earned them the title the 'Lions Comiques'.

These two performers were to lead the way in the 1870s. Previously, comics had predominantly portrayed characters who were down-at-heel, or had adopted various roles by simply changing their hat or coat. Leybourne and Vance, however, would completely change costume and countenance for each of the fully formed characters that they portrayed.

The Great Vance was born Alfred Peck Stevens in 1839. His working life began as a clerk in a London solicitor's office, not a career for which he had a particular ambition. The regular pay-cheque, however, guaranteed a few good nights out at the singing saloon.

He was a well-dressed gent for these bawdy houses, and his sense of fashion meant he stood out like a toff amongst his fellow working-class spectators. He carried himself with elegance and ease and the ladies frequently vied for his attentions. It was his personal appearance that initially motivated his first steps towards the limelight; capitalising on his boyish good looks, he created a successful routine as an early female impersonator. To add variety to his act, he also blacked-up and performed minstrel routines with his brother, but his success was secured when he adopted the character of a rich fop about town, a more natural progression for such a fashionable young man.

Vance's toff was an elegant chap with a monocle, a gold-topped cane, a solid gold toothpick and daringly tight trousers, which were the subject for much mockery by other comics. His new character swaggered onto the London stage in 1864 and was an instant hit. The lyrics of his songs contained a lot of nonsense and his voice was criticised for its nasal tones, but the public loved his tunes and sang them outside the halls, many a factory ringing with the derivative melodies and his frequently risqué lyrics.

Vance's popularity extended to the patronage of the Prince of Wales (Edward VII), who lavished expensive gifts on the star. Vance was by now becoming a real-life version of the mashers he parodied. He gained a reputation for eating huge quantities of cockles and whelks, which he washed down with champagne. In fact, he claimed to drink champagne 'as a working man drinks beer, by the pint in a pewter pot'.

In 1872, Vance toured in Scotland and made his first appearance at Britannia. The audience was not the most receptive to his foppish antics, which appeared more suited at that time to the London stage. Although this first appearance did not receive the usual acclaim his performances met, eight years later he returned, and this time Britannia rang with his praises:

> At 9 o'clock the Great Vance received the greatest ovation on record.
> On Monday the Great Vance's programme was thoroughly enjoyed.
> A pleasing entertainment by an artist of undoubted merit.
> There is only one word for Vance – he is GREAT!'

For 24 years the Great Vance toured Britain, receiving a rousing welcome wherever he went. But like so many of his contemporaries, he was a victim of his own success; the years of constantly racing from engagement to engagement and the effort spent in keeping his public happy had taken their toll. His career and life ended on Boxing Day 1888 when he collapsed whilst waiting in the wings of the Sun Music Hall in Knightsbridge.

George Leybourne created a whole world of foppishness. Born Joe Saunders in Newcastle in 1842, he began his working life as a hammer-man (a metal worker). He first began performing in the East End of London under his real name, but as his act developed he changed it to the more suave George Leybourne.

His first big break happened when he was engaged for a year at the Canterbury Music Hall. The manager had been impressed by the young man's act and before long Leybourne was earning £25 a week. Among the first of his successes was the cockney song 'Hit him on the Boko, Dot him on the Snitch', which was a tribute to the adventures of Tom Sawyer. This number was soon eclipsed by the instant popularity of his song 'Champagne Charlie', which he performed resplendent in his Piccadilly weepers, the name for his moustache:

I've seen a deal of gaiety throughout my noisy life
With all my grand accomplishments I ne'er could get a wife,
The thing I most excel in is the P.R.F.G. game,
A noise all night, in bed all day, and swimming in Champagne.

Chorus:
For Champagne Charlie is my name, Champagne Charlie is my name.
Good for any game at night, my boys, good for any game at night, my boys,
Champagne Charlie is my name, Champagne Charlie is my name.
Good for any game at night, boys, who'll come and join me in a spree?

The way I gain'd my title's by a hobby which I've got,
Of never letting others pay, however long the shot,
Who ever drinks at my expense are treated all the same;
From dukes and lords to cabmen down, I make them drink Champagne.

Chorus repeats

From coffee and from supper rooms, from Poplar to Pall Mall,
The girls on seeing me exclaim, 'Oh! what a champagne swell!'
The notion 'tis of ev'ry one, if 'twere not for my name,
And causing so much to be drunk, they'd never make Champagne . . .

His earnings suddenly shot up to £125 per week and 'Champagne Charlie' became his signature tune. William Holland, the manager of the Canterbury, gave George a carriage and four horses to embellish his debonair persona and advertise his act. Holland also insisted that he drink nothing but champagne when he was in public. The song was to make Leybourne a household name and also gained George a sponsorship deal with Moët and Chandon to promote their product. Part of the payment was huge quantities of the bubbly drink, and this was perhaps one of the first recorded incidents of celebrity endorsement.

Leybourne believed the secret to his success was that he was the most handsome man on the British stage and certainly one of the tallest as well. He would perform his act with apparently little effort, his melodious voice seducing the ladies in the audience, who would then swoon if he winked in their direction. His stage presence was matched by his talent as a songwriter and he wrote the words to many of his own songs, especially the ones he is best remembered for today including 'Champagne Charlie', 'If Ever I Cease To Love', 'Up in a Balloon Boys' and 'The Man on the Flying Trapeze', which celebrated the sensational debut of Leotard the trapeze artist, who, without a net, flew over the heads of the audience at the Alhambra, a small music hall attached to the back of a pub in the Isle of Dogs.

> Whoa! He'd fly through the air with the greatest of ease,
> A daring young man on the flying trapeze.
> His movements were graceful, all girls he would please,
> And my love he has stolen away.

On Monday 13 June 1881, the Britannia advertised the 'important engagement of the Great Lion Comique, Mr George Leybourne'. At this time Leybourne was one of the highest-paid and hardest-drinking men on the British stage. Throughout the week-long engagement the superstar quaffed so much champagne and beer that the stage-hands had to practically carry the man up onto the stage, to the immense hilarity of the audience who evidently thought it was part of the act.

The 1880s saw the two Lions Comiques not only reach the height of their popularity but also of their rivalry. The battling comics would send up each others' acts. For example, when Leybourne was having a great success with 'A Dark Girl Dressed in Blue', Vance countered with 'The Fair Girl Dressed in Check'. On another occasion Vance caused a sensation with his song about zoological gardens called 'Walking in the Zoo' – the song popularised the word 'zoo' as an abbreviation to the mouthful 'zoological garden'. George countered with a song about a visit to the aquarium called 'Lounging in the Aq', though it failed to have the same impact on the English dictionary as Vance's little ditty.

Without doubt, Leybourne was one of the great comics of his day and, as with many funny men, off-stage he suffered badly from depression. Near the end of his life he became completely withdrawn and it would take considerable persuasion to encourage him onto the stage. Once confronted by the audience, however, he would shake off his despair and become once again the lively, champagne-swilling swell the crowd had always loved. He drank himself to the grave, dying in Islington in September 1884, and leaving his wife and two children without a penny.

In 1944 Tommy Trinder and Stanley Holloway brought the Lions Comiques back to life in the film *Champagne Charlie*. The film is heavily criticised for inaccurately portraying the famous pair, but it gives a true flavour of what life must have been like in the Victorian music halls as this would still have been strong in the memories of the filmmakers.

Illustrated front page of 'Walking in the Zoo' sheet music

Illustrated front page of 'Lounging in the Aq' sheet music

THE LADIES COMIQUES

The 1870s and 1880s saw female patter comediennes and singers topping the bill in the leading music halls. These were the bravest women of the stage as they relied on their quick wit and swift turn of phrase as their only shields and weapons against the ferocious audiences that could smell fear a mile away. Amongst the most noted who appeared at the Britannia were Miss Bessie Bellwood and Miss Jenny Hill.

MISS BESSIE BELLWOOD: THE SLANGING SERIO

Bessie Bellwood was born in London in March of 1856, and was christened Catherine Mahoney. Her parents had been from County Cork and, like thousands of other Irish folk, had fled their home in the 1840s, when the potato blight meant that food, work and money were in desperately short supply. Catherine was bought up with her two sisters and two brothers in a good Irish-Catholic household. Mr and Mrs Mahoney were determined that their children should grow up to be proud of their Irish heritage. From infancy, Bessie had listened to her parents singing the ballads of her ancestral home and as soon as she could sing the airs herself, she would beguile her family with her juvenile renditions.

Her early working life was spent in a factory in Bermondsey where she spent long hard days skinning rabbits and dressing the pelts. Near the factory was the Star, an old Free-and-Easy-style music hall which offered plenty of opportunities for brave amateur acts. She had always been told what a wonderful voice she had and knew that it could be the key to a better life. As life as a rabbit skinner was a far worse prospect than any horror the audience of the Star could offer, she stepped onto the stage and performed as an Irish singer.

As debuts go it probably wasn't the worst, but the audience lived on a diet of comic songs and sketches; Irish ballads weren't quite to their taste. However, she survived the ordeal, undeterred from her goal to become a performer.

Her first few attempts on the stage were to help develop her act. Her ballads were generally heckled. Bessie, however, was not going to take the abuse lying down, so she started to argue and banter with the audience. Before long she dropped the Irish routine and opted instead for a line in cockney song. However, it was the patter she added between the verses and her slanging matches with the ever-vociferous music-hall audience for which she is famed. Once she had a five-minute slanging match with an enormous coal man, the pair of them arguing back and forth with quick, razor-sharp witty insults and verbal abuse. At the end, Bessie was victorious and the coal man left embarrassed and demoralised as the audience laughed and mocked him in his crushing defeat.

Bessie was not stupid: although she used 'slum slang' during her act and sometimes played the dumb broad, she was in fact able to take on any audience, on any subject, with her razor-sharp wit and quick tongue. The audience adored her for it. In November of 1881 'Bessie Bellwood, the unrivalled lady comique' appeared in Britannia, where her colourful patter crammed with saucy innuendo both shocked and impressed the crowd; she was the embodiment of the spirit of the music hall.

She may be regarded as a patter comedienne rather than a singer, but her songs were known across the country. The most famous included, 'He's Going to Marry Mary Ann', 'What Cheer Ria', 'Woa Emma!' and 'Aubrey Plantagenet'.

In 1884, as she was reaching the height of her career, Bessie married a commission agent from Leeds named John Nicholson. The couple seemed happy enough whilst courting, but after the wedding the groom disappeared and was not seen again until Bessie's funeral, when he made a bold appearance.

For most of her life Bessie appeared as an independent woman of her own means, and she consorted with many wealthy and aristocratic people. But it was not status that she was after; she courted these people to help with her own good causes, as Bessie had never forgotten, nor even left behind, her humble roots. She helped the poor and needy in any way she could: she tended the sick, did laundry and cleaned in the most desperate of homes and she constantly tried to raise funds for the poor. Her own upbringing had been poor, but her parents had been generous with what they had, and so would she.

Her good Catholic upbringing stayed with her throughout her life and privately she rarely exhibited the bawdy behaviour of her public reputation, although it did occasionally spill out. On one occasion, for example, she had, over the course of a couple of hours, been in a very serious and devout conversation with Cardinal Manning in regard to raising funds for charity. Within minutes of leaving the cardinal, she was arrested on Tottenham Court Road for hitting a cabman and knocking him down because she thought he had insulted the man she was in love with. Bessie achieved her ambition to be a star of the music hall, and that success was rewarded with several shows a day, six days a week. Any time she had to spare was spent working tirelessly to help those who needed it most. On 24 September 1896, at the age of 39, she died. Her death certificate stated the cause of death as 'Cardiac Disease Exhaustion'.

JENNY HILL: THE VITAL SPARK

London, not surprisingly, was the birthplace of many music-hall stars and our next, Jenny Hill was also born in that city, in 1851. She was christened Elizabeth Pasta. Her father was a London hackney-carriage driver who numbered amongst his passengers many celebrities of the London theatres and music halls. Perhaps it was seeing these well-dressed, well-paid artistes that inspired him to place his little girl upon the stage. In the 1860s, Jenny made her debut as a child performer singing comedy songs at the Doctor Johnson Concert Room in Fleet Street. She was a pretty little girl who even at an early age knew how to work the crowd, able to make them laugh and cry.

As she grew up, her voice gained her regular spots in the smaller London halls, but she got her first real break when she was given the opportunity to sing in the London Pavilion. She was an instant success and soon gained herself a reputation as a 'serio' (a serio-comic), described in an advertisement for Britannia as 'the most artistically, realistic, comic and pathetic singer on the music hall boards'.

From the start, her stage act was lively and bubbly. She could be saucy, cheeky and funny, or pathetic and tragic, depending on what the song demanded, but the act was always delivered with enormous energy. Her lively on-stage persona gained her the nickname 'The Vital Spark'.

Her beauty didn't go unnoticed either and she cultivated many male admirers, some of whom were so enchanted by her they would unhitch the horses from her carriage and pull her home themselves.

Her fame made her one of the earliest pop stars, with thousands of people buying the sheet music for the songs she made popular. Jenny is perhaps best remembered for the song 'The Boy I Love is up in the Gallery' which, in March 1882, featured as a part of her act in Britannia. As the song was already quite well-known, the audience sang along and waved their hankies as her clear voice chimed, '*The boy I love is up in the gallery, / the boy I love is looking down at me. / There he is, can't you see, waving his handkerchief, / as merry as a robin that sings in the tree.*' Her comic turn was just as warmly received and local critics declared that in her performance at the Britannia she had lived up to her billing as 'the leading star seriocomic artiste of the day'.

Like her contemporary, Bessie Bellwood, Jenny was literally worn out by the demands of her busy life. She died aged 44.

Britannia in the 1880s

MRS ROSSBOROUGH ALONE

In 1889 Mr Rossborough died after 20 years of running Britannia Music Hall. His widow carried on his work and continued to supply a bill of fare which the public adored. Mrs Rossborough was a rare lady. There were a few other women in business, certainly, but they didn't command the same respect as men, and they certainly didn't flaunt their positions of power. During the 1880s and 1890s, women began to emerge slowly from the shadow of their male counterparts, prompting disgruntled resentment from many men. One local bard wrote:

We've women doctors, women lawyers, women this and that,
They've started wearing trousers, and dress wi' a tile hat;
At fitba,' cricket, or cycling, they'll challenge ony men,
Whit this world is coming tae, I really dinna' ken.

From this simple chorus it is obvious that Glasgow in the 1890s was still a long way from female equality.

In the music halls, although it was common practice for the wives to do much of the book-keeping and administration, it was quite unusual for them to openly run the whole show. At this time, however, Glasgow had two lady proprietors in the same neighbourhood. Around the corner from the Britannia the Scotia Music Hall was also being run by a widow, Mrs Baylis, who, like Mrs Rossborough, had worked with her husband for most of her married life. Whether or not these two ladies sought each other as friends is not recorded but they would have certainly known each other as they were rival managers. However, the rivalry that had always been hospitable between the two music halls and these two women would have had plenty to talk about as well as very similar burdens to share. Mrs Baylis struggled on with the Scotia until 1890 when H.E. Moss (of Moss Empires fame) took over. Mrs Rossborough continued until 1892 when it simply became too exhausting for her to manage anymore. She hung up her manager's hat and handed over Britannia to the eager young William Kean.

10 MR WILLIAM KEAN PROUDLY PRESENTS

William Kean had his finger on the pulse of the latest trends in entertainment. As the new century drew nearer, the air was full of the promise that new technologies offered. Entertainment teetered on the edge of these advancements and, although Britannia was still boasting a respectable audience and all the leading stars, it wasn't packing them in the way it used to. Kean knew the building needed to be brought into modern times.

Unlike most wooden music-hall auditoriums which were burnt to the ground as a result of smoking and the prolific use of naked flames, Britannia did not have a fire in the auditorium throughout her history as a working music hall. It has often been speculated that the lack of toilet facilities might have been an effective method of fire prevention. Nonetheless, in 1893, within a few months of buying Britannia, Kean added a men's toilet. (The ladies didn't get one, it appears, until the 1920s.) Britannia did, however, remain fire-free after the installation of toilets – perhaps it was simply laziness that kept the wooden hall moist. This could also be another explanation for the fly buttons beneath the balcony.

During the few years that Kean was the proprietor, he continued to provide the customary mix of burlesque performers, comics, dancers and singers. He also provided more in the way of novelty and speciality acts, including the acrobatic Lizette Troupe; Haig and Haig, Knockabout acrobats; the Mikidios, double-telephone-wire performers 'who were expert on their wires'; the Voltynes, 'exceedingly clever in their triple, horizontal bar performance'; Professor Dremain with his 'Electricone' – 'a brimful of novelty and has only to be seen once when the spectator has the desire to witness it again'; Marvello, the 'prince of jugglers and balancing with lighted lamps'; Mr Ludwig Linu, whose 'contortionism is very wonderful and leads me to doubt whether he has any bones at all'; and Sir Daniel Sullivan, who could 'lift a dog-cart in which four persons are seated, and the horse that draws it, clear off the ground by the power of his teeth', who was rivalled a few weeks later by the appearance of Monsieur De Saivin, who showed off his odontological prowess by lifting 'a large barrel with 32 gallons of water and two heavy men sitting on the barrel stride legs, with his teeth'. Conjurers included Dexteria and George Douglas, 'Mirthful Mystifiers'; Vosper the 'Necromancer'; Professor Allan McCaskell, 'Humorous wizard', and Mademoiselle Leoville, the only lady conjurer who topped the bill with critical success, newspapers reporting that for 12 nights she had astonished the audience by her sleight-of-hand work and was applauded nightly. On the same bill Professor Le Wist, 'the singing ventriloquist, mimic and polyphonist' was advertised. The list of performers engaged is extensive and Kean was continuously on the look out for some new novelty. He also engaged some of the most frightening acts.

Victorian acrobats, similar to those
who performed at Britannia

THE GHOST SHOW

Séances were huge business in the music halls in the late nineteenth and the early twentieth century. In 1895, Britannia boasted Professor Holmes and Madame Lena who 'gave a séance which surpassed all others seen before'.

This revival in the fashion for contacting the dead came to Britain from America where the Fox Sisters and Madame Blavatsky were astounding the public with their incredible psychic abilities. Although originally these attempts to contact the dead occurred in private rooms and parlours, theatrical managers soon saw the potential for presenting this act on the music-hall stages. However, the traditional parlour routines where the participants would sit around a table, join hands and ask questions such as, 'Is anyone there? Knock once for yes and twice for no,' did not easily translate to a hall filled with 1,500 very lively spectators. This meant that the 'mediums' employed would be forced to use all sorts of tricks to create ghostly manifestations and ensure the audience was not disappointed.

Amongst the most famous illusions used by Professor Holmes and many others is 'Dr Pepper's Ghost', where a disembodied spirit would, when summoned, walk across the stage in all its transparent glory. This illusion was achieved with the use of cleverly placed mirrors which would reflect an actress waiting back stage in her nightie. When prompted, she would drift past the mirrors and her ghostly form would appear to float across the stage.

Another trick was the famous spirit cabinet, into which an alleged member of the audience would be placed, with hands and legs tightly bound so that they could not 'fake' the ensuing phenomenon. The medium would then coax the volunteer into a hypnotic state and the cabinet's curtain would be closed. The auditorium would become silent; all chewing, talking and coughing stopped as the watching audience sat on the edge of their seats in anticipation. Suddenly the building tension would break as objects – plates, cups, balls and tambourines – were thrown violently into the audience from behind the curtain. Then, as suddenly as the onslaught had started, it stopped. The curtain was pulled back and the volunteer revealed still tightly bound and still in the depths of their hypnotic trance. There was only one explanation: the ghosts did it.

The use of ectoplasm also became a popular feature of these wonderful ghost shows. The medium, deep in a trance, would start to manifest a spirit which would appear in his or her mouth. An assistant would then proceed to pull the glowing, luminous ectoplasm out of the medium's mouth, very slowly so that the audience could get a jolly good look at the manifestation. The ectoplasm was created using cloth soaked in phosphorus which would glow eerily and very brightly in the darkened auditorium. It is likely that this practice did nothing for the medium's breath or health.

Provoking spirits wasn't necessarily all smoke and mirrors though; mediums also did a booming business contacting the departed relatives of members of the audience. Some of these mediums were fakes who would use their abilities to read people, fishing around the audience for names, looking for reactions from individuals they could home in on and to whom they could 'pass on' a bogus message. Sometimes, though, the messages were so specific to the people they were directed to that it was hard to refute that some of these psychics were genuine.

Men of science and learning, men generally regarded as being far too rational to believe in such ethereal things, had a few ghost-show fans in their number. Sir Arthur Conan Doyle, John Logie Baird (who had lived and worked only a few hundred yards from the front door of Britannia), Marconi and Thomas Edison were among the late nineteenth- and early twentieth-century celebrities who were fascinated by these amazing manifestations and messages. Baird himself started to experiment using images and sound which he would send across space. These experiments eventually became the basis for television.

Marconi, when experimenting with radio signals, was stunned to receive signals from a completely unknown source. He spent the last few years of his life trying to perfect a machine that could communicate with the 'other side'.

Sir Arthur Conan Doyle, another fan of this strange and enigmatic style of performance, would visit spiritualist churches and music halls and would attend private readings and meetings in his pursuit of the truth. In fact, it became somewhat of an obsession, for which he also received a fair amount of criticism.

Whether you believe in ghosts or not, one thing is certain: ghost shows were an imaginative and often spectacular addition to the bill, and there are popular rumours of ghosts inhabiting the building today.

W.F. FRAME: THE PHUNNIEST OF PHUNNY PHELLOWS

Although it seems that Kean was in constant pursuit of the most unusual acts, he still also continued the tradition of booking the biggest and best names in the business. One such celebrity was W.F. Frame, who was always guaranteed to pull in the crowds. When he appeared on Britannia's bill of fare on 24 May 1893, the *Evening Times* reported: 'streams of people could be seen flocking in, the evening house was packed'.

He was known for his humorous ditties, catchy speech, and quaint characters which often brought down the house.

His career began in 1867 when he appeared for the first time in Glasgow's Scotia Music Hall. The crowd there was a tough audience to please, but during the course of his engagement he managed to win them over and before long he was booked in the all the popular Glasgow houses. Frame's act was one of the first to parody the Scots. He bounded about the stage dressed in a kilt that exposed his knobbly knees as he portrayed a cheery wee chap, as endearing as he was funny. He soon earned the affectionate billing 'The Man U Know'.

Like many of his contemporaries, pantomime was to feature in W.F. Frame's career. His first role was playing the dame Maggie Mucklemoo in *Goody Two Shoes* at the Royal Princess's Theatre in the Gorbals. This show was a huge success, and he was a regular of the pantomime world from then on. He loved playing the dame, but after a few years he decided he would like to play the villain. In 1892 he took on the role of Uncle Abanazar in

Postcard illustration of W.F. Frame

Aladdin. Whilst performing the role on stage, Frame was hit by a bottle which had been lobbed from the gallery by an over-excited young man. Not wanting to lose one of the stars of the show, the manager jumped onto the stage and squinted into the full force of the stage lighting. He was unable to spot the culprit, so instead announced a £5 reward for any information as to his identity. The young man, however, was not found.

W.F. Frame toured with his own company throughout the 1880s and 1890s, performing across the UK, including in Britannia. In 1898, he travelled to America, where British music-hall stars were warmly welcomed (as long as their act remained within the realms of decency).

One of Frame's most famous songs was 'Tommy's Got the Money'. It included a couple of verses and choruses with patter written by Alex Melville, who also penned some of Harry Lauder's numbers. The patter section of the song was vital to the comedy of the number. For example, in the first verse, Frame, playing the part of Tommy, sang:

Never was so happy in all my life,
It's no' because I have got a ducky o' a wife,
It's because my uncle died, tae make the matter clear,
An' left me a fortune o' twa hunner pounds a year.

He would then launch into a patter section:

I got a new rig-out for 13 shillings and 6d and then I went doon to see ma dov', Sairah Square-face. She's a grand singer Sairah. She wis singin' 'Flora Macdonald's Lament' when I went in and it wis the most lamentable thing I had ever heard in all my life. Johnnie Bluelugs was there an' he's an airn [iron] grinder and Sairah's mither was there tae, she asked me when I was going tae marry her dochter. 'Weel,' says I, 'say a fortnight.' 'You're in a hurry,' says the old wife. 'Maybe,' says I. 'But whit way dae ye want tae be married in a fortnight?' 'Oh,' says I, 'just because –'

Tommy's got the money he will cut a dash,
Tommy's very funny when he's got the ready cash,
Tommy Twin has got the tin, he'll spend it never fear,
An' be a ladies' masher for twa hunner pounds a year.

This song was a resounding success and hot on the heels of Frame's popularity emerged other 'Scotch' comics, the most famous of all being Harry Lauder, who is discussed in more detail later in this book. Lauder may well have been inspired by W.F. Frame's routines, but Frame was never a fan of Lauder. Overshadowed by the young comedian's success, he criticised Lauder and when he made a splash in the London halls, W.F. Frame countered by ensuring his own engagement in the English capital and writing his billing himself:

> Frame's a wee bonnie laddie. He has come from the Brighton hippodrome to the London Alhambra and the sprig o' heather crowns his cap. Frame is as famous as the Macgregors – his name is a household word from John o' Groats to the farthest corner of the Scottish dominions. His quaint conceits, his inspiriting work refreshes us like a breezy blow in the top of Ben Nevis. Assuredly the most comical fellow we have seen in London since Frame came here before.

In London, Frame's humour was well enough received, but his use of Scots made it difficult for the English audience to understand a lot of the gags. Lauder, on the other hand, had realised this and had modified his act to accommodate the English ear. Of course, Lauder is still remembered today, while few people outside of Scotland have heard of W.F. Frame, who, in his early years, earned himself the sobriquet 'Phunniest of Phunny Phellows'.

HARRY CHAMPION: 'BOILED BEEF AND CARROTS'

William Kean also presented Harry Champion, 'comedian and singer of racy songs', in April 1893.

Champion was born in London in 1865 as William Henry Crump. From childhood he had shown the deep joy he gained in making people laugh. He wrote little routines which he performed for his parents, and he clowned around for his classmates. After leaving school, Harry turned down an apprenticeship with his father (who was a cabinet-maker) in favour of a life as a comic. His parents, though encouraging, insisted that he also found himself a trade, so he headed for the bright lights of the variety stage, stopping off at a cobblers on the way to sign up to an apprenticeship.

In 1882, aged 17, he was given his first chance to perform at the Royal Victoria Music Hall in Bethnal Green. He was to be billed as Will Conray and as he approached the theatre he was full of the confidence of youth. After ten minutes in the hall, though, reality hit home. The audience was in an abusive mood, and, after listening to heckling and jeering, the lad was a nervous wreck. When his name was called, he refused to go on, and the manager quite literally had to shove him on stage, where he nervously began his well-rehearsed routine. By the end of the act, his confidence had returned and the manager offered him a week's trial. Still warm with the roar of his first applause, he boldly asked the manager for a pay of £10 a week. The manager looked at the boy. 'One pound, lad, that's enough for you,' he said and Harry, quite wisely, accepted.

He stayed on the bill at the Victor for a full month, after which he headed to Marylebone where he had secured a month's contract. At this time, Harry was still officially apprenticed to the cobbler so he could only work at the music halls part-time. This meant that although he was developing a good act he was unable to make the best of his talents. At last, sometime in 1886, his apprenticeship ended and he was released from his servitude. After that, nothing could stop him.

By now he had developed a black-faced routine where he would sing a popular song as a white man and then quickly black up and carry on, singing a plantation number. With his apprenticeship finished he found himself re-engaged to play at the Marylebone Music Hall where the manager, Mr Botting, had expected a reprise of his old material. Harry, however, wanted to try out his new routine, which he was sure would meet with his employer's approval. The act went down well enough with the audience and he was well applauded, yet as he stepped off the stage Botting sacked him. It transpired that he was not a fan of minstrel acts, of which, he thought, there was an overabundance in all the halls. Harry was not one to give up, however. He knew that Botting was a stubborn man, so rather than argue for another chance, he simply changed his stage name from Will Conray to Harry Champion and returned with a different act as a quick-fire comic. With this routine he managed to finally win over Botting.

In 1889 Harry married his sweetheart Sarah Potteweld. Sarah became not just his wife, but also his manager. She was quite a shrewd businesswoman, but did not see any great income from her husband's theatrical exploits. What she did notice was the amount of money he spent on carriages to convey him from music hall to music hall, as he performed in

The exterior of the Britannia Panopticon today, as seen from the Trongate

View of the Britannia Panopticon auditorium from the proscenium arch

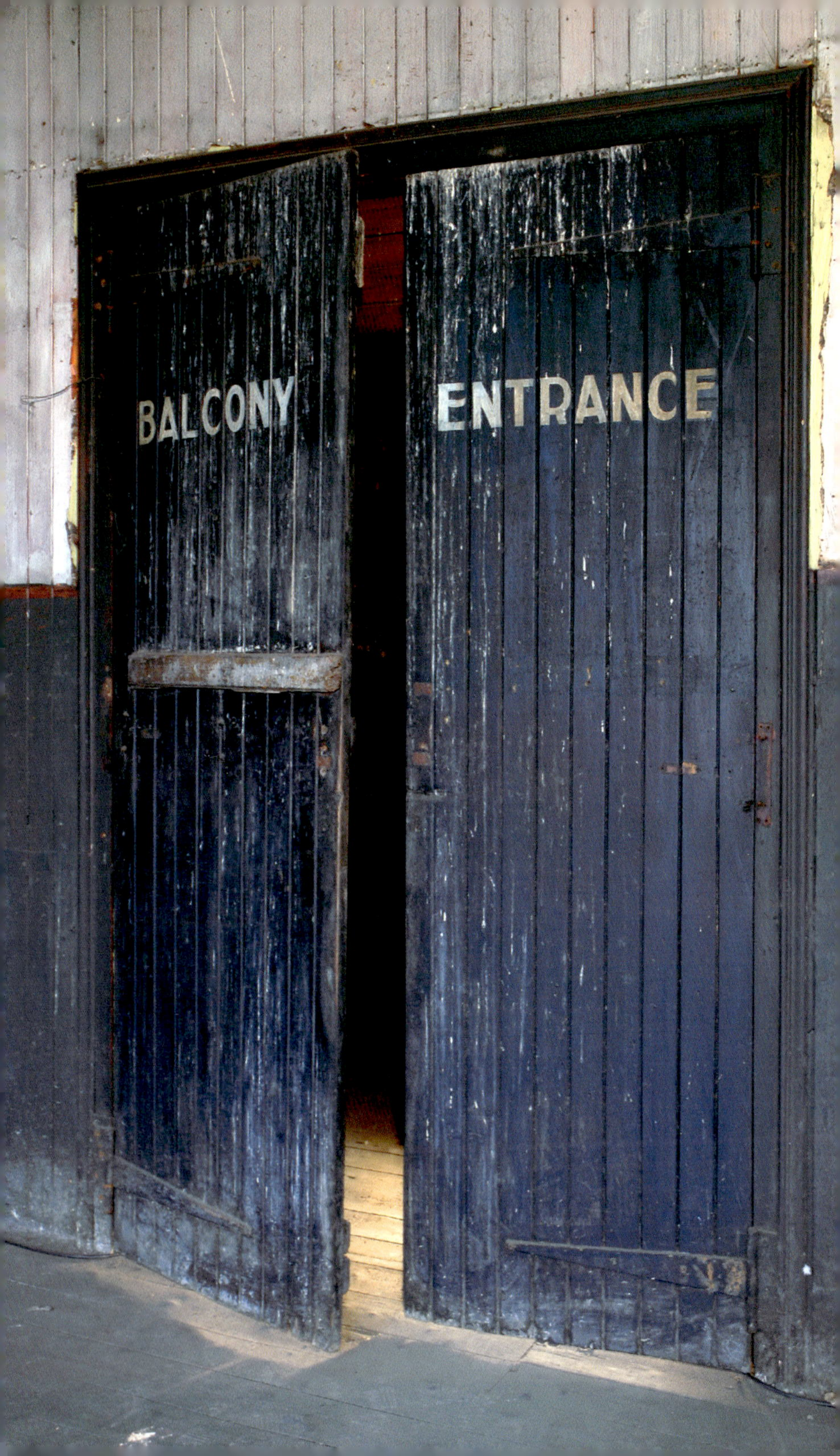
BALCONY
ENTRANCE

(Opposite) The entrance to the balcony

1920s exit sign above the balcony doors

View of the Britannia Panopticon auditorium from the balcony entrance

One of the ceiling arches, with peeling layers of paint, and gold stars underneath

(Opposite) View of the balcony and ceiling from the proscenium arch

A selection of artefacts found in the Britannia Panopticon

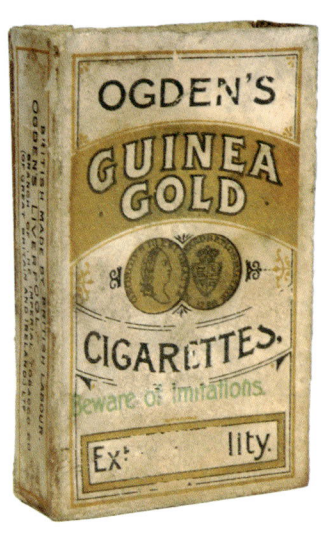

Britannia poster from 1896 advertising the Four Daisies act

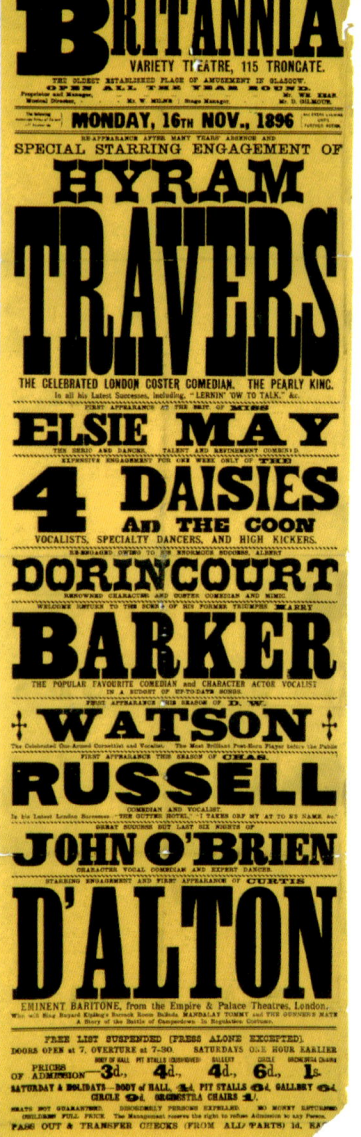

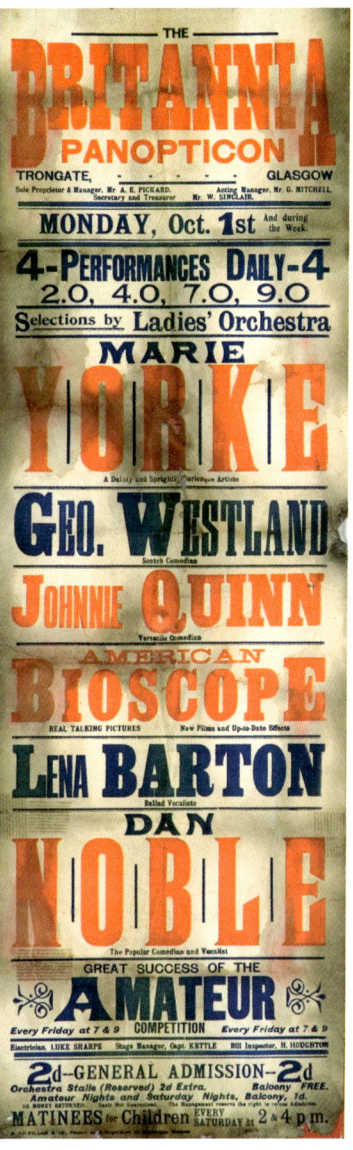

Poster (c.1906) found underneath the carnival floor

Britannia programme from Arthur Hubner's era

Front cover of a Panopticon programme (*c.*1911) found under the balcony floor

Back cover of the programme, showing A.E. Pickard

Poster (*c.*1915) found under the carnival floor, which depicts a rescue from a fire

Large two-part poster (c.1906) found under the carnival floor

Cover illustration from the sheet music of 'Champagne Charlie', George Leybourne's hit song

Pickard's Museum poster advertising Solomon

(Overleaf) Poster advertising Harold Pyott ('Tom Thumb')

HAROLD PYOTT
TOM THUMB THE 2ND

AS HE APPEARED WHEN ON EXHIBITION IN SOUTH AFRICA

SMALLEST ADULT HUMAN BEING THAT EVER LIVED.

WITH ALBERT BROUGH THE ENGLISH GIANT.

Postcard of Stan Laurel and Oliver Hardy, signed by Stan Laurel

Judith Bowers as 'Florrie Bow Wow' in a recent show at the re-opened Britannia Panopticon

three or four a night. Harry defended himself by stating that all music hall performers relied on horse power to get them to their various engagements. Sarah therefore bought him a brougham, which they hired out to other performers as well, making a good deal of extra cash in the process.

As the years moved on, Harry's act evolved into what became a very fast-paced comedy routine in which he would rattle through songs at high speed, his tongue cleverly managing to get around every word. This super-quick delivery became his trademark. The 1890s saw Harry touring north of the border, and in 1893 the Britannia audience gave the pithy songster a hearty welcome. They loved a tune they could sing along with, and, after his week-long engagement there in 1893, the Trongate most likely rang with his songs.

By the time the First World War arrived, his songs were known in every household and included 'A Little Bit of Cucumber', 'Any Old Iron', 'I'm Henery the Eighth I Am' and 'Boiled Beef and Carrots'. He became so famous for this last tune that London restaurateurs would simply put the name 'Harry Champion' on the menu to describe that popular dish. However, it is 'I'm Henery the Eighth' which is best remembered today:

You don't know who you're looking at; now have a look me!
I'm a bit of a nob, I am, I belong to royaltee.
I'll tell you how it came about; I married Widow Burch,
And I was king of England when I toddled out of church.
Outside the people started shouting, 'Hip hooray!'
Said I ,'Get down upon your knees, it's Coronation Day!'

Chorus:
I'm Henery the Eighth I am!
Henery the Eighth I am, I am!
I got married to the widow next door,
She's been married seven times before.
Everyone was a Henery;
She wouldn't have a Willie or a Sam.
I'm her eighth old man named Henery,
I'm Henery the Eighth I am!

I left the 'Duke of Cumberland', a pub up in the town,
Soon with one or two moochers I was holding up the Crown.

I sat upon the bucket that the carmen think their own;
Surrounded by my subjects I was sitting on the throne.
Out came the potman, saying, 'Go on, home to bed!'
Said I, 'Now say another word and off'll go your head!'

Chorus repeats

Now at the wax-work exhibition not so long ago
I was sitting among the kings, I made a lovely show.
To good old Queen Elizabeth, I shouted 'Wotcha Liz!'
While people poked my ribs and said, 'I wonder who this is!'
One said, 'It's Charley Peace!' and then I got the spike.
I shouted 'Show your ignorance!' as waxy as you like.

Harry was an enduring star of the music-hall stage. Even after music hall had gone into decline in the 1930s, he still did his best to entertain and performed with Florrie Ford, Charles Coburn, Marie Lloyd Junior and even the Crazy Gang. His CV also included three Royal Command performances and three feature films: *On the Air* (1934), *Equity Musical Revue* (1935) and *Old Timers* (1936), in which he co-starred with Lottie Lennox, Marie Lloyd Junior and Charles Coburn.

In 1942 he died, aged 76, of nervous exhaustion bought on by work. His funeral was a private affair attended by his children and grandchildren. He was laid to rest in the same plot as his beloved wife, Sarah.

THE MARVEL OF THE NINETEENTH CENTURY

In the early spring of 1896, William Kean closed Britannia for several months in order to modernise the building. Teams of workmen – upholsterers, carpenters, painters and electricians – descended upon the place. The installation of the electrical supply was a truly revolutionary advance: at this time only 301 premises in the City of Glasgow had the electric light, which cost 6d a unit to run. Electricity was modern to the point of being futuristic, dragging the world out of the gas-lit shadows of the early industrial age.

When Britannia reopened on 25 August 1896, a new entertainment dominated the bill.

The following matchless array of talent will appear
TO-NIGHT (TUESDAY), 25th August, 1896,
And every evening Until Further Notice.
GRAND COMPANY for the RE-OPENING.

~

Mr Kean has much pleasure in announcing that during the recess
the entire Building has been painted and re-decorated, Upholstered, and a
complete installation of the electric light throughout the entire building.
The following Tradesmen have carried out the various contracts:–
Painting and decorations, John Sweet, 88 Great Western Road:
Upholstering, Archd. Stewart & Sons, Union Street; Electric Light, W. G.
Higgs & Co., 88 York Street.
The Whole under the supervision of Mr. Kean.

~

First appearance at the 'Brit', for one week only of
THE CINEMATOGRAPHE
or ANIMATED PICTURES
The Marvel of the Nineteenth Century.
They will nightly give selections from the following Pictures:–
The Blacksmiths' Forge, Comic Scene at a Restaurant, Cock Fight,
Mexican Duel, Rescue from a Fire, Boxing Match, Buffalo Bill,
Lynching Scene, Japanese Dance, The Prismatic Skirt Dance by
Loie Fuller as a finale each Evening.

Postcard illustrating a skirt dancer

The projectionist and supplier of this entertainment was a man called Arthur Hubner who, at that time, was the manager of the Skating Palace on Sauchiehall Street. Hubner had started showing moving pictures in May and had had a profitable run with them. This success had not gone unnoticed by Kean who was keen to exploit this new technology, though tentatively at first, not entirely sure that his audience would appreciate the silent flickering films. Magic lantern shows had always proved popular in the past, and in the February of the previous year 'living pictures' were shown using a version of the biograph, an American device which worked on the same principle as a flick book, where a series of consecutive images printed onto card and shown in quick succession give the illusion of motion. Photographic cards were placed around the outside of a drum and this was placed inside a box which also contained mirrors and a lens. When the drum was quickly turned, the resultant moving images were projected onto a screen. The audience were mesmerised as 'the celebrated Tableau Vivants, an entirely new series of beautiful and artistic living pictures' came alive before their eyes'. Would they receive this latest advance with the same enthusiasm?

Hubner was a firm fan of the moving-picture business; he could see potential in these films, as well as the benefit of recording life in Scotland at that time. His passion for this new art led him to become one of the first movie cameramen of the city, as well as one of the first projectionists. His cinematic debut in Britannia was, as he predicted, a resounding success, as the following report in the *Daily Record* (29 August 1896) illustrates:

Great Success of
THE CINEMATOGRAPHE
Supported by the best company in Glasgow

Money was refused at the Britannia last night. No more need, therefore, be said about the size of audience, which, from beginning to end of an excellent programme, was kept in boisterous good humour by an array of talent which reflected credit on the selection made by the manager. The songs and dances of McQue and McKay, the performances of 'The Mikidios' and the Irish ditties and dances for which Geraghty and Gilligan were responsible, were each enthusiastically applauded, and the rest of the items on the bill of fare provided a thoroughly 'Guid Nicht'.

Illustration of Arthur Hubner on a poster

By the end of this first week, so many people had been turned away because of the cinematograph's popularity that it was decided to re-engage the films for an extra week.

At first it must have seemed that cinema was just another novelty that would tour the halls for a couple of years, after which some other new innovation would appear to take its place. It seems, however, that both Hubner and Kean had foresight, confident that one day moving pictures would be more popular than the music halls and church halls in which they had been shown.

In January 1897, Hubner took over from William Kean as the manager of Britannia Music Hall, film now being a regular feature of Britannia's playbill. Arthur Hubner offered an ever-changing programme of the latest films and variety turns, ensuring that Britannia remained one of the most popular places for entertainment in Glasgow.

⓫ MR ARTHUR HUBNER PROUDLY PRESENTS

Electricity may have meant better lighting and the advent of cinema, but the benefits to entertainment did not end there. A flurry of new acts using electricity in their sketches in one form or another appeared. The most famous to appear in Britannia was Dr Walford Bodie, MD.

THE ELECTRICAL WIZARD OF THE NORTH

Bodie presented himself like the legendary Mephistopheles: he was a slightly frightening and very exotic character with raven-black hair, piercing dark eyes and a moustache waxed and twisted so that each end stood almost perfectly erect. His wicked look would both seduce and terrify the ladies. In real life, Bodie lived quietly in his humble home, which was, as one would expect, a castle.

He was born Samuel Murphy Bodie on 11 June 1869 near Aberdeen. Both his parents were ordinary church-fearing folk who had aspirations for their son to train as a minister. However, in this brave new world of electricity, he was not for the doctrines of God and instead sought employment at the local telephone exchange, where he could learn more about the telephone and electricity – two hugely modern inventions at the time. He was fascinated by the

Postcard of Walford Bodie

telephone and wrote a book on the subject, and he even invented appliances such as a phone that would automatically ring when a fire started in the house.

Outside of telephony his hobbies were magic and ventriloquism, pastimes which would lead him to tread the boards for the first time in Stonehaven town hall at the tender age of 15, relying on his talent for showmanship. During his first show he performed a very skilled magic act, followed by his ventriloquist routine. However, when he performed the following week, he gave a presentation about South Africa, which was surprising as, at this point, he had never left Scotland. His confident and assured delivery, combined with his precociousness, appears to have entertained the audience anyway.

At around about this time, Bodie also began to develop an interest in what can be most accurately described as quackery. At the age of 17, he claimed to have had his first success as a healer. This was an interest he was to pursue for the majority of his career and it was also to get him into trouble, repeatedly.

In 1890 he became fascinated by the newspaper reports on the execution of the murderer William Kemler in Sing Sing Prison. Kemler's demise left his name indelibly printed in the history books as the first victim of the electric chair. People were horrified as they read the descriptions of the final death throes caused by electrocution. For Bodie, on the other hand, these reports rekindled his interest in electricity, and he set about building a replica of the infamous electric chair. Assisted by his wife, Jeannie, billed as Princess Rubie, Bodie perfected a routine which was to take the music halls by storm.

A report in the *Glasgow Herald* at the time described the act: a volunteer would be plucked randomly from the audience and placed in the chair. They would first be hypnotised so that they wouldn't feel any pain and then the electrical current would be switched on. 'When the volunteer's face turned black, the electrical current was switched off and with the vigorous use of slapping the volunteer was again revived.'

At this point, Bodie was still only 21.

In 1897 he took up the job as assistant manager of the Connaught Theatre of Variety in Norwich. The manager was his sister's husband, H. Werner Walford, for whom Bodie had a respect so great that he took his name for his stage persona. Bodie quickly discovered that his greatest strength lay in being on the stage. His act by this time included magic, mesmerism, ventriloquism, telepathy (which included a mind-reading routine with his wife), clairvoyance and hypnotism. He had also added the letters MD after his name.

Electricity played a huge role in his act from then on, his time working at the telephone exchange finally paying off. At the end of 1897, Bodie's act appeared on the bill in Britannia. The audience was mesmerised as he performed daring electrical experiments assisted by the lovely 'La Belle Electra'.

Bodie stepped out onto the stage dressed in cloak and top-hat, with his moustache waxed in his now customary manner. He stood with his arms dramatically thrust up into the air as La Belle Electra attached electrodes to his body. Members of the audience were then selected to join the great man on the stage. Most approached apprehensively, fearing perhaps both the devilish-looking man and the torturous-looking electrical apparatus. Suddenly Bodie would nod at Electra, who would pull down a huge lever, switching on the current. Bodie gritted his teeth, flung his head back and tensed his body as thousands of volts of electricity coursed through him, his fingertips appearing to crackle with blue lightning. The volunteers standing beside him felt the current tingle through their own bodies, causing their hair, to the hilarity of the watching audience, to stand up with static charge. Next, Electra would invite a courting couple on the stage and ask them to kiss. The couple would hesitantly approach each other, but as their lips drew closer, electric sparks would pass between them, preventing the pouting lips from touching. The audience loved it.

Bodie also became famed for his healing powers and his use of 'Bloodless Surgery', a combination of hypnotism (which he preferred to call Bodic Force) and manipulation. Bodie would pass an electric current through his body and his own hands into the affected area of the patient. The patient would then exclaim in astonishment that his ailment had gone. The patient was always alleged to be a volunteer from the audience, but many spectators had their doubts. Bogus or real, Bodie received some attention as a healer – perhaps there was something in what he was doing. Whether he was genuine in his interest to research and produce healing benefits from electricity or whether it really all was just an act, he did develop 'electric medicines', including Electric Life Pills, Electric Liniment and Bodie's Health Spa, which he sold with some degree of success.

By 1906, Dr Walford Bodie MD was commanding a weekly fee of £400 per week and had added several other letters after his name. He boasted numerous degrees and qualifications in his publicity, but his success and fame meant that he was now making enemies – namely the entire medical profession. They thought that the fraudulent doctor was dangerous and was making a mockery of real medical practice. Furthermore, his successful showman quackery endangered those members of the public who might take it seriously. Bodie endeavoured to justify his qualifications and issued a statement in which it was claimed he had gained his degrees from 'Barrett College' and 'Chicago College of Medicine', both in America, and that he had studied further in Paris and Vienna. He backed up his credentials with graduation photographs of himself wearing his academic robes. Bodie found himself in court asked to justify the title of MD which he had quite patently given to himself. When he explained that the initials merely stood for 'Merry Devil', the case was discharged.

He was not so lucky with other cases bought against him. On one occasion he was ordered to pay a huge fine after he failed to impress the court with a demonstration of his 'Death Cage Experiment', or with his long list of qualifications, which, it transpired, he had acquired from a dentist in Bradford, Yorkshire.

Bodie wearing academic robes

It was soon after this case that, in November 1909, Bodie was to make a return visit to Glasgow to perform more feats of electrical magic, this time at the Coliseum. Bodie had adorned the outside of the building with walking sticks, crutches and all sorts of medical aids, allegedly discarded by the satisfied public that he had healed.

The medical students at the University of Glasgow were incensed by this display and turned up en masse on the opening night; they began by hurling verbal abuse at the man, and then threw eggs and pease meal at him on stage. Bodie retaliated with pointed and

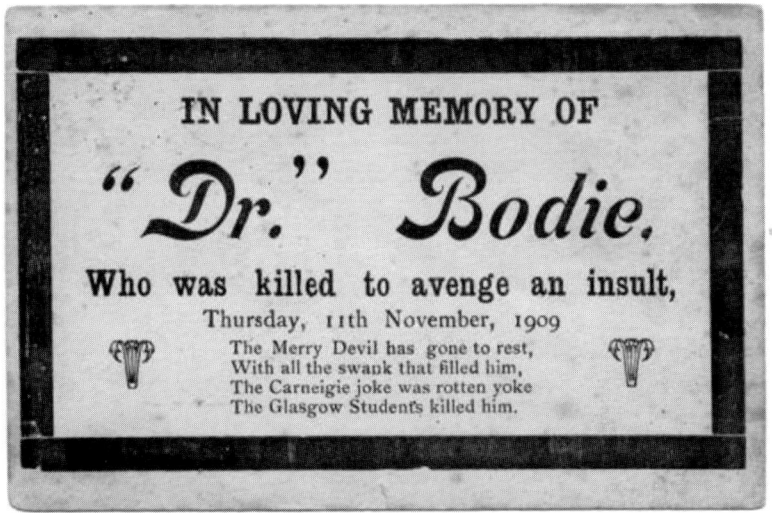

IN LOVING MEMORY OF

" *Dr.* " *Bodie,*

Who was killed to avenge an insult,

Thursday, 11th November, 1909

The Merry Devil has gone to rest,
With all the swank that filled him,
The Carneigie joke was rotten yoke
The Glasgow Students killed him.

Promotional postcard documenting the student riot against Bodie

cutting insults directed at the students who made up over half of the audience. On the following night the same thing happened and by the third night Bodie was warned that further demonstrations by the students were being planned. Come the fourth night, the police were in the theatre waiting for the promised trouble to start. A thousand students turned up (many from universities out with Glasgow) and positioned themselves in the circle. When the curtain came up and Bodie appeared on the stage he was greeted with every kind of missile imaginable, including eggs, fruit, vegetables and rotting herrings! The frightened orchestra members fled the pit and the fire curtain came down; the manager feared for the safety of his auditorium, which was being seriously damaged during the riot. The students demanded an apology from Bodie, which he duly tried to provide, but he could not be heard above the fracas and shouts of 'Charlatan!'

The police eventually managed to move the rabble out of the Coliseum, arresting several of the ring leaders, but much of the mob continued the demonstration by heading to the West End of the city and attacking the premises of two other known quacks.

One of the ring leaders, incidentally, was a young student named Osborne H. Mavor. He subsequently gave up medicine in favour of play-writing, changing his name to James Bridie, and eventually founded the first college of drama in Scotland.

A week after the Bodie riots, the Glasgow Empire Theatre advertised a parody of Walford Bodie called 'Dr Awful Bogie', an act which burlesqued Bodie's electric and mesmerism acts.

With the Glasgow students' taunts of 'Bodie Bodie, quack quack quack' still ringing in his ears, Bodie cancelled many of his following engagements. It had been the worst year of his life, with huge court costs, a nightly assault from a Glasgow audience and, on top of this, the tragic death of his 18-year-old daughter in the summer of that year. When he finally did regain the courage to brave the stage, he was afforded a warmer reception and continued his career with some degree of success. One of his great comforts was his wife, Jeannie, and his son Albert, who seemed destined to follow in his father's footsteps as a talented illusionist. However, Bodie's luck was still on the downwards spiral: Albert died in 1915, aged 26.

Both Bodie and his wife believed that hypnosis could be a useful tool in both preventing and solving crime. It is interesting to note that although Bodie might have been regarded by many as a charlatan, his interest in using science to heal and to solve crime was genuine and he was always reading and researching the latest advances in the scientific world. He also wrote a number of books himself, including *The Bodie Book*, *Valuable Prescriptions* and a detective novel entitled *Harley the Hypnotist*, which received some acclaim, and was even favourably compared with Sherlock Holmes.

Although his medical expertise was somewhat wanting in both qualification and proven success, Bodie's inquisitive and adventurous spirit lead him to such exotic terrains as India and Ceylon, where he sought out the answers to many an old trick and a few new ones as well. Once he investigated the truth behind the Indian Rope Trick, only to come to the conclusion that the trick had either been misreported or invented by a drunken sailor. He interviewed and met up with magicians from all over the world, writing copious notes about his discoveries. Sadly, these notebooks were destroyed when the ocean liner on which Bodie and his troupe were travelling was hit by a torpedo. He wasn't the luckiest traveller, it seems: another ocean voyage also resulted in torpedo attack, after which Bodie decided to stay in Britain and travel by rail instead. Trains, however, also proved a precarious means of transport – he was once travelling in a train when it derailed.

Despite the mishaps that befell him, Bodie was certainly one of the most flamboyant showmen of his age. He was a great self-publicist and he performed before packed houses wherever he went – even if much of the audience consisted of sceptics or enemies. His act was now a mixture of healing, illusions and scientific novelties, which he toured with his own company of variety artists. For a time the company included a young Harry Lauder; in fact, Bodie could be said to be responsible for Harry Lauder becoming one of the highest-paid performers of all time. Lauder was earning £4 10s working for Bodie, but when Bodie persuaded the theatre agent Foster to see the young Scot at work, Foster landed Lauder with the contract which was to catapult him to stardom.

By the 1920s, people were more familiar with electricity and were no longer so astounded by the antics and experiments Bodie provided. Jeannie, his wife and assistant of 40 years, died in 1931, and he married a young dancer a year later. In 1939, now an old man, but with a twinkle still in his eye, he was performing at Blackpool Pleasure Beach when he tragically died of a perforated gastric ulcer.

HARRY LAUDER: 'THE END OF THE ROAD'

As Bodie's career floundered, the career of his protégé, Harry Lauder, reached its peak.

The eldest of eight children, Lauder was born in his grandparents' cottage in Portobello, near Edinburgh, on 4 August 1870. Rather scandalously, however, his parents only married, on the 26th of the same month.

Lauder was brought up to believe that he was a descendant of one of the fourteen sons of Sir John Lauder, who in turn was a descendant of the Earls of Lauderdale, who were descendants of Sir Robert de Lawedre, who had helped Malcolm Canmore recover the Scottish crown from Macbeth. In fact, Harry Lauder's family were simple, plain, poor, hard-working folk. His grandfather was a joiner and his father a potter.

In 1877, after a brief time in Musselburgh, the family moved to Glasgow. Their stay in Glasgow was also short-lived as Harry's father, who was very skilled at his work, was offered a better position in a pottery near Chesterfield. It seemed for a few months that the family was finally entering more prosperous times. However, as in any good tale, disaster was just around the corner. Harry's father, John Currie Lauder, caught pneumonia and died.

Harry's mother, Isabella, had been left with eight children. She had no way of supporting them in Derbyshire, so had no choice but to move back to Scotland, where she had family in Arbroath. The years that followed were tough for the young Harry. His mother's income alone could not feed her brood, so Harry, who was only about 12 years old, went to work in Gordon's flax mill. He worked 12 hours a day on Monday, Wednesday and Friday as a 'towie', collecting the tow as it passed through the heckling machine and pressing it into a receptacle (usually a sack). This was monotonous and dangerous work and Harry carried scars from being caught in the machinery for the rest of his life. It taught him to be quick on his feet, however, and it earned him a bit of money. On Tuesday, Thursday and Saturday, he went to school in the mill grounds.

At the age of 14, Harry's uncle Sandy managed to get him a job in the Eddlewood Colliery near Hamilton in Lanarkshire. His whole family moved with him and they all squashed into Uncle Sandy's rather small house. Harry's work at the pit brought in a respectable 9 shillings or more a week, and he became quite good at his job. It was arduous, however. Long hours underground in cramped, cold and damp conditions took their toll, not just on the men, but also on the pit ponies that pulled the coal cutches (wagons) below ground.

Harry grew very fond of the sturdy little ponies and when he moved to another colliery, he became a pony driver. His little pony was called Captain, and the two became the closest of friends. On one occasion, Captain even saved Harry's life when his highly tuned pit-pony senses detected that the tunnel was about to collapse and Harry was able to escape.

Harry must have wished that he could have taken Captain with him when he moved jobs, for, a few months later, at another colliery, he and several others were trapped for 18 hours after a roof collapsed.

Harry worked hard and, when his younger brother joined him in the mines, the two of them gained themselves quite a reputation. They were nicknamed the 'Coal Mawks', and between them they earned over five pounds a week.

Throughout his childhood, Harry's main social activities had centred around the Band of Hope (a Temperance movement) and the Salvation Army. At these soirées, Harry was able to vent his pent-up talents as a

Harry Lauder in his 'Feather in Glengarry' costume

comic singer and meet his sweetheart Annie (whom he always called Nance). The couple married in 1891. On their wedding day, Harry, in true comic fashion, forgot the ring. Other than that, it was the perfect day, followed by a romantic honeymoon in Glasgow and a visit to Macleod's Waxworks on the Trongate.

By now, Harry was very much in demand at the Band of Hope meetings and it dawned on him that he could charge a fee for his performances. His popularity with these genteel audiences secured him £1 per performance. In 1892 he entered a comic-singing competition which was being promoted by the Glasgow Harmonic Society, another Temperance movement. He won second prize, and further bookings for his talents soon came flooding in. He began to create stage characters, adopting a costume of paisley shawl and elastic-sided boots, and founding what would become his signature act.

Mrs Baylis of the Scotia Music Hall in Glasgow gave the young Harry his chance on the professional stage. The audience was as notoriously difficult to please as that of the Britannia, but he sang two songs and survived. Mrs Baylis, however, told him to 'gang hame and practice.'

Undeterred by Mrs Baylis's advice, Harry set off on a 14-week tour with a travelling company around the smaller towns of Scotland. The tour was successful, but not profitable, and, with a wife and young child to feed, Harry returned to the coal mines. He never gave up his dream of becoming a performer, however, and his talents had not gone unnoticed. J.C. Macdonald, a well-known comedian in Scotland at the time, had his own touring troupe and he offered Harry a job. Harry signed a two-year contract with Macdonald, and even though the pay was much less than that of a coal miner, he embarked on a ten-week tour of the north of England. Although this work was not as well paid, he loved performing and was gradually building a name for himself. Annie supported his ambition and made do with whatever money her husband bought home.

After a successful tour with Dr Bodie, Harry secured himself an agent, and by the end of 1896 he was being paid £6 a week. During this time, Harry had become great friends with a fellow performer and violinist, MacKenzie Murdoch. They decided to form their own concert party and tour Scotland. Sadly, it was a financial failure and they lost £100 in the first year. Subsequent tours, however, were more successful, and by 1897 Lauder was getting a good billing in the music halls, including the Britannia, where he was performed solo. Harry's week-long engagement at the Britannia was never mentioned in any of his reminiscences, though he fondly remembered many other halls. Legend has it that the Britannia audience seemed to have given him a rather cool reception, preferring instead to reserve their appreciation for the alluring Tessie Vandean and the enchanting Sisters Morgan, with whom he shared the bill.

Finally, in 1900, Harry made his first London appearance, in Gatti's music hall at Westminster Bridge, where he absolutely delighted the audience with his quaint Scottish characters. This engagement was to be the first of many and he was soon an established star of the London stage.

In about 1902, Harry decided to make use of the new technology for recording the voice, the Edison-Bell cylindrical record. By this time, well used to receiving huge bursts of laughter from the audience, he didn't expect the silence he got from the machine at the end of his number. The silence went on and on as Harry wondered where the applause was; then he finally remembered that he was singing to a machine. He suddenly burst out laughing and fell off the stool he was sitting on, ruining the recording in the process.

By 1911, Harry was earning up to £5,000 a night. This wasn't quite the happy ending to his story, however; Harry still had tragedy to face. On New Year's Day, 1917, Harry received a telegram from the War Office telling him that his son, Captain John Lauder, had been killed in action. Harry was devastated. In all his life, he had never suffered so much as he did then. Torn apart by grief, he carried on, throwing himself into war work and entertaining the troops in the trenches – a very dangerous occupation. His song 'The End of the Road' became a standard of the First World War, and was a song of hope and courage for the servicemen. It could just as easily have been a theme tune for his life.

Every road through life is a long, long road,
Filled with joys and sorrows too,
As you journey on how your heart will yearn
For the things most dear to you.
With wealth and love 'tis so,
But onward we must go.

Chorus:
Keep right on to the end of the road,
Keep right on to the end,
Tho' the way be long, let your heart be strong,
Keep right on round the bend.
Tho' you're tired and weary still journey on,
Till you come to your happy abode,
Where all the love you've been dreaming of
Will be there at the end of the road.

With a big stout heart to a long steep hill,
We may get there with a smile,
With a good kind thought and an end in view,
We may cut short many a mile.
So let courage every day
Be your guiding star alway.

Chorus repeats

In 1919, his work entertaining the servicemen was rewarded with a knighthood, and from then on he was known as Sir Harry.

Sir Harry's singing voice was regarded as one of the best in the business. Chaliapin, the great tenor, said that if he wanted to hear a perfect singing voice he would put on Harry Lauder. This was a factor, however, that few of his audience seemed particularly to care about, as it was Harry's hilarious characters and his portrayal of a funny wee Scotsman in kilt and bonnet that they loved.

In February 1950, Sir Harry suffered a severe stroke and died at his home, Lauder Ha' in Strathaven, Lanarkshire. Britain mourned the loss of this star of the music halls.

Sir Harry's songs, including 'I love a Lassie', 'A Wee Doch and Doris', 'Roamin' in the Gloamin'' and 'Stop Yer Tickling Jock' can, however, still be heard sung in the streets of many Scottish towns, especially at Hogmanay when the 'old yins' have had a wee tipple.

Postcard of Harry Lauder

CHARLES COBURN: 'THE MAN WHO BROKE
THE BANK AT MONTE CARLO'

Charles Coburn is believed to have spent some time in his youth growing up in Argyll, but generally he was regarded as a cockney singer, his place of birth being Stepney. He was born Colin Whitton McCallum in 1852 and made his debut as Charles Coburn 20 years later at the Alhambra. He had a moderate amount of success in the halls of London, earning enough to keep heart and soul together, but his was not to be a swift rise to stardom.

In 1879, he briefly gained himself the title 'Comic of the Day' for his six-month billing at the Oxford, and earned a respectable fee, but it wasn't until 1886 that he was to perform a song which would rise to the top of the music-hall charts.

He had heard a ditty called 'My Nellie's Blue Eyes' being sung on the stage of a hall in which he was appearing near the bottom of the bill. The tune was a catchy number but the words were awful. Unable to get the tune out of his head, he began to compose a new set of lyrics, replacing his Nellie's blue eyes with 'two lovely black ones'. With his new song in hand, wearing a costume of a faded, worn-out coat and with both of his eyes blacked out, Charlie made his way to the Paragon where his 'Two Lovely Black Eyes' was an instant hit, audience members presumably empathising with the lyrics: *Two lovely black eyes, / Oh what a surprise, / Only for telling a man he was wrong, / Two lovely black eyes.'* Coburn certainly appreciated the song's success, as his name finally made it to the top of the bill again.

It was five years, however, before he was to repeat the success of this song. Although he had a vast collection of equally good, if not better, melodies, his 'Two Lovely Black Eyes' had made an indelible mark on the British public and the refrain could be heard in pubs and homes across the country. His second hit, when it finally came, had an even greater impact.

In 1891, Charles first performed 'The Man Who Broke the Bank at Monte Carlo'. This song told the story of a lucky chap who wins big money in the casinos of the glitzy resort. It was allegedly based on the true story of a con-man who really did 'break the bank' in Monte Carlo. Whether the story was true or not, the song certainly improved Coburn's own bank balance. Coburn later claimed that, over the years, he had sung 'Monte Carlo' 250,000 times, in 14 different languages.

In August 1893, he decided to return to Scotland, the home of his ancestors. He was engaged to perform in Britannia, and, as his two hit songs were already well known, thousands turned out to see him. In September, Coburn was still performing at Britannia. Beneath a notice which read 'New Kissing Packet, contains full instructions on how to kiss, when to kiss, where to kiss. Also twenty opinions of the press on Kissing. Sent post free – 2 stamps' an advertisement for Britannia appeared: 'Mr Coburn still tops the Bill.'

By the end of the 1890s, Charles Coburn had all but disappeared from the stage, partly because he failed to have another hit, but also because of his reputation as a slightly shady and unpleasant character, which ensured the London music-hall managers didn't trust him. In 1894, his London career had almost come to an end when he had offended the management and owners of the Palace Theatre of Varieties with his tactless song 'I've Never Turned Money Away', in which he parodied a Jewish man. The Jewish owners of the theatre were not impressed, and, after that night, Charles Coburn found it hard to get good work in the capital, his reputation having taken a serious blow.

In additional, his personal life was tainted by his association with some rather dubious characters, including the infamous murderer, Dr Crippen. It appears that Coburn had first met Crippen when he had been working with the minor music-hall star, Belle Elmore – Dr Crippen's wife. It also appears that Coburn had known Ethel le Neve, Crippen's girlfriend. When Crippen was finally arrested and executed for the murder of his wife, the case was so famous that a shadow was cast over the reputation of everyone associated with the man, including Coburn.

With work in London dried up, he travelled instead to the towns and cities in the north, where he was always assured an appreciative audience. In 1903 he revisited Britannia, which promoted his billing as a 'return to the site of his first Scottish success'. As with his first appearance, crowds flocked to see him and he signed 1,000 copies of his song sheets for the gathered crowd. He rarely appeared on the London stage again, although he did perform in the line-up at the end of the Royal Music Hall Command Performance in 1912.

Eventually, after years of making the odd guest appearance to sing his two most popular numbers, Charlie made a small outing into the world of cinema, appearing in the little known British film *Variety Jubilee* (1943). He died two years later and the film disappeared into the archives. His name is largely forgotten today, but his hit song, 'The Man Who Broke the Bank at Monte Carlo' lives on:

I've just got here, thro' Paris, from the sunny southern shore;
I to Monte Carlo went, just to raise my winter's rent.
Dame Fortune smil'd upon me as she'd never done before,
And I've now such lots of money, I'm a gent.
Yes, I've now such lots of money, I'm a gent.

Chorus:
As I walk along the Bois Boolong,
With an independent air,
You can hear the girls declare,
He must be a millionare,
You can hear them sigh and wish to die,
You can see them wink the other eye,
At the man who broke the bank at Monte Carlo.

I stay indoors till after lunch, and then my daily walk
To the great Triumphal Arch is one grand Triumphal march,
Observ'd by each observer with the keenness of a hawk,
I'm a mass of money, linen, silk and starch.
I'm mass of money, linen, silk and starch.

Chorus repeats

I patronised the tables at the Monte Carlo hell
Till they hadn't got a sou for a Christian or a Jew;
So I quickly went to Parie for the charms of mad'moiselle,
Who's the load-stone of my heart. What can I do?
When with twenty tongues she swears that she'll be true?

Chorus repeats

12 THE BOYS IN THE BALCONY

With the turn of the century, Britannia remained a popular house for the delinquent boys of the East End, who flocked to the music hall and crammed themselves along the benches in the balcony, as close to the front as they could manage. They particularly seemed to favour the section of balcony hanging over the front of the stage. Here the performer was exposed to the boys, who would urinate over the edge of the balcony in an attempt to hit the act below. Horse manure freshly scraped from the cobbles was a popular alternative to urine, creating a lovely and satisfying splat when properly aimed. The boys in the balcony have left behind a small collection of their possessions including tin whistles, bits of spinning-tops, catapults, rubber balls, marbles and initials carved into the wood.

One account from 1903 tells the story of the ladies' orchestra which was also at risk from the boys in the balcony. The ensemble was advertised as a Japanese orchestra of geishas, and it numbered four ladies (all from the exotic East End of Glasgow), who prayed that the boys had full bladders, for if they did not, there would not be enough water pressure to hit the comic on stage and the urine would instead trickle onto them in the orchestra seats, dribbling down their black geisha wigs.

Bad behaviour was not a new problem; a civic investigation in 1875 into the need for stricter regulations in music halls outlined the often scandalous content of the programme and concerns about the amount of children who were exposed to it: 'If you were to witness the effect produced upon the young girls and boys who, in large numbers, flock to the cheaper class of those scenes of pollution, it would require no further argument to prove what a bane and curse they are to the population of this great city'.

In addition to the moral effects of music-hall entertainment, the physical effects on children were also highlighted. One investigator for the *North British Daily Mail* noted the 'insufferably offensive' smell of the music halls, 'caused by certain conveniences in constant use, without water, and in a filthy condition'. Pipe-smoking and 'the offensive exhalations' added to the unhealthy environment – a music hall, he declared, was 'a very hotbed of disease'. He also calculated that there were 'at least 2,000 [children] under 13 and 5,000 from 13 to 17, in the regular habit of attending these places of amusement . . . about three-fourths are boys and only one-fourth girls.'

It was recorded that 50,000 or so children between 13 and 17 years of age were known to live in Glasgow at that time, with only 554 attending any of the 'evening schools' of the city. Evening schools had been provided so that children could go to work during the day and receive some instruction in reading, writing, numbers and religion in the evening. In an attempt to prevent Glasgow's children from going off the rails completely, the civic investigators suggested that better evening schools be provided, with science and dance added to the list of activities. These new, improved evening schools would look after and influence the children, and teach them to 'despise the low character of the amusements which at present attract so many of them'. The fact that by the age of 13 children were often expected to work the same long hours as their parents meant that many had lost interest in the idea of school and turned instead to the music hall for their edification.

In the early years of the twentieth century, the cultivation of gang culture amongst the boys gave them a new outlet for their high spirits. Many people have an idea of Glasgow as being quite a rough old town with a history of gang violence. Every large city in Britain at this time had its rough areas, and the history of the gangs isn't unique either, but somehow Glasgow gangs became the most notorious. Two of the most famous gangs of the early twentieth century, both of them from Glasgow, were the San Toy and the Tongs.

Surprisingly, these two gangs reflect one of the biggest news stories of the day, the Boxer Rebellion in China, where rebel forces comprising of Chinese peasants fought against the tyranny and change brought by foreign influence in trade, religion, politics and technology. The Boxer uprising began in November of 1899 and raged until September 1901, the rebel gangs making world news as they attempted to thwart Western intervention and fervently protected their independence. The new railway was a main target of the rebels, and, as the troops tried to advance along the railroad to Beijing, the rebel forces waited in Tong Tcheou, where they achieved their greatest success in pushing them back, notching up a good few casualties in the process.

This civil war inspired the writing of an operetta entitled *San Toy*, which featured in the music halls of Glasgow in about 1901. In turn, these events and the operetta served to be an inspiration to the young men of the city who named their gangs the San Toy, after the operetta, and the Tongs, after the rebel triumph at Tong Tcheou. These gangs were (and still are) rivals. It appears that Britannia was the territory of the San Toy, as 'San Toy Boy' is carved very clearly into the front of the balcony.

Toys left behind by the boys in the balcony

13 ALBERT ERNEST PICKARD

At the end of 1903, it appears Britannia closed whilst vital works in the interest of public safety were carried out. Essentially, a new staircase and a door at the stage side of the auditorium were added for the purposes of evacuation in the event of a fire. During the auditorium's closure, Hubner's interests turned to the management of his two other houses, the New Eastern Alhambra and the Alexandra Music Hall in the Cowcaddens (which he renamed the Royal Music Hall). When Britannia finally re-opened in 1905 there was the name of a new lessee above the door: Mr James Anderson.

16th January 1905
Britannia Music Hall
Lessee – Mr. James Anderson. Manager – Mr. Harry Hemfrey
Musical Director – Mr. H. Taylor
Most expensive engagement of WARNER AND WILSON
The Up-to-date comedians direct from London

RYDER DAVIS character comedian
EVA WARD Comedienne
JACK McCORMICK the funny chap
ALICE GOLDING Ballad Vocalist
THE BRANSBYS Character Duettists and comedy entertainers.
McFARLANE The Dancing Marvel
NORMAN BROS Equilibrists, Hand-balancers and Acrobats
SIMS, DALY & SIMS In their great speciality act, Juggling with Clubs etc.
BIOSCOPE.
By Special Request Mr. James Anderson will give his entertainment entitled
A NIGHT IN IRELAND
Look out for Great AMATEUR WRESTLING COMPETITION
commencing Monday 23rd Jan.
Prizes, £5, £2, and £1
Amateur night every Friday
Always a great success!

Together Anderson and his manager, Harry Hemfrey, did their best to keep the old Brit alive in the wake of the modern halls which had recently opened, including the Pavilion, the King's Theatre and the Coliseum. It was obvious, however, that Britannia could no longer compete, and at the end of 1905 management was again to change, Hemfrey having been offered opportunities in pastures new. James Anderson found himself in need of a new manager and, fortunately for both him and Britannia, the right man was close by. He was the new proprietor of the neighbouring museum and waxworks, a young man with a strong Yorkshire accent by the name of Albert Ernest Pickard.

Albert Ernest Pickard (or simply A.E. to his friends) was born in Bradford in February 1874. His early life is something of an enigma and his later life of his own invention.

Some accounts state that his family had made their money in the Yorkshire cotton mills, a wealth that seems to have vanished by the time A.E. had come along; it is believed the young lad had started his working life as an engineer's apprentice at the age of 10. And that's about all that can be said about his early life, other than the fact that from an early age he showed great imagination and ambition. These attributes meant he felt the boundaries of his home town confining him like prison bars. He was desperate to get away from the dark, Victorian grimness of Bradford and travel the world. Life as an engineer's apprentice did not promise the adventure, excitement and opportunities he craved, so he left home, rarely mentioning his former life again.

He exchanged one apprenticeship for another when he was taken on by a travelling show to learn the tricks of the trade of one of the most up-to-date fairground attractions of the day, the 'electric rifle range'. This experience was to determine the course of his life. At the fairground, he learnt how to 'spiel' by watching the other stall operators shouting catchy phrases that extolled the virtue of their particular game or entertainment and attracting the pennies of passers-by. It was not a job for the shy and retiring. Competition between the rival pitches was often fierce and Pickard paid attention to every trick, exploit and gimmick the veteran showmen used. His apprenticeship served him well and, after working with a rifle range in London for a while, had saved enough money to buy his own range, to which he successfully applied all he had learnt, managing to create a lucrative little business. It was obvious from this early success that he had an innate ability as a showman.

During this time, the young lad ventured to see P.T. Barnum's travelling show. Barnum was to be this young lad's biggest inspiration. He was enthralled by the immense variety of entertainments found in the various wagons, tents and booths: side shows, freak shows, animal acts, fairground games and novelties galore, all crammed to bursting with an eager audience. This sort of show had been going on for centuries, but, with characters like the larger-than-life Barnum, Bailey and Buffalo Bill, travelling shows had encountered a revival in the late nineteenth and early twentieth centuries. Barnum had become particularly famous for his American Museum in New York, where all the latest novelties, waxworks and side shows were viewed daily, all under the one roof. The reputation of his museum in New York preceded him to Britain, where his shows drew enormous crowds as a result.

After a successful spell running his rifle range, Pickard managed to amass quite a tidy sum of money for himself and decided to invest it in an American Museum of his own. But where was he going to open his house of fun? London would be the most obvious place, but that city was far too expensive, with far too much competition, and Bradford was a place he didn't wish to return to. Instead, he set his sights on Glasgow, a city which had a reputation as an entertainments centre second only to the English capital.

He arrived in Glasgow in 1904 and spent every penny he had saved on buying an old waxworks museum, Fell's Waxworks, at 101 Trongate, at the corner with King Street, and just two doors east of Britannia. The museum was a run-down relic from an already by-gone era full of strange novelties which had long since passed into the realms of antiquity. He renamed the venue the American Museum and Waxworks, unashamedly cashing in on Barnum's well-known establishment. With little cash left to renew and update his exhibits, Pickard instead used his imaginative publicity skills to ensure that a constant stream of visitors filled the place. Downstairs in the small foyer he placed an automaton, a mechanical dummy or scene which, when a penny was placed in the slot, would come to life and entertain the viewer for a few brief moments before again becoming still. This popular exhibit, which, according to legend, was a red-faced laughing man or a cavalier, tempted the visitor to spend the extra 2d admission to the floors above, which the advertisements promised were filled with the largest selection of exhibits in the city. Children in particular flocked to see the various displays and spend what little money they had on the penny machines within.

A TOUR THROUGH PICKARD'S MUSEUM

Sadly, the American Museum (which was also known as the British Museum, and as Pickard's Museum and Waxworks) does not remain in the magnificent state of preservation that Britannia does, but fortunately there are a few descriptions of it which have survived.

In July 1935, the *Evening Times* featured an article about the museum in which the writer reflects upon the strange exhibits to be seen at the waxworks at 101 Trongate: 'For a penny you could watch the death agonies of a man lying in a glass case. According to the notice – "To see the painful moving of the eyes and the heaving of the chest place a penny in the slot."'

For the more refined, their penny would perhaps have been better spent in a machine called 'What Jones Saw in Paris'. In return for the penny, the viewer would be treated to a tour around some of the art treasures of France's capital.

According to the article, industry was represented by 'the World's oldest sewing machine, rusty and dilapidated, which was said to be worth a thousand pounds. The "works of art" include Dr. Pritchard and his Wife (Pritchard having been the last man to be publicly hanged in Glasgow), a Chinese torture chamber, the Destruction of Jerusalem, and a 5,000 year old Egyptian mummy.'

Perhaps the best description of the museum can be found in a catalogue which Pickard produced in around 1911 (and a copy of which is retained in the store for the People's Palace in Glasgow). In it, each floor of the museum is described in detail with regards to the exhibits and paintings on view. The collections to be seen were so varied that there was something of interest for everyone that visited. Even today's blasé public would have found plenty to gawp at.

Set out over four floors, the museum could be accessed from the street via a spiral staircase which led the viewer up through the building. On every floor, vast rooms contained a variety of objects, ranging from the bizarre novelties, which were always popular, to the more intriguing artefacts from important moments in world history. He promoted the collection as belonging to 'The Most Up-to-date Museum in the World'.

Starting from the Trongate entrance, the visitor was directed past a large automaton in the foyer, which was always surrounded by the eager faces of grubby children. The visitor would then find themselves mounting the staircase to the various floors. On the journey up the spiral stairway that led to the first room, the visitor would pass a 'photogravure' of His Majesty King Edward VII, in masonic regalia. Upon entering the first room, the visitor was treated to a number of further portraits and models in wax of members of various royal families and many notable characters from British and world history: Queen Victoria, the Queen Mother Alexandra, George V, Queen Mary, HRH The Prince of Wales, HRH Princess Henry of Battenberg and various other princes and princesses, who shared the space with an old enemy, Napoleon Bonaparte.

Military and political leaders were also well represented, including Lord Roberts, Lord Kitchener, Admiral Togo, Lord Rosebury, Lord Charles Beresford, Right Honourable Joseph Chamberlain and Li Hongzhang (a leading statesman in China, who had died in 1901). These notable characters sat cheek by jowl with such unusual persons as Old Malabar (a Glasgow street entertainer, who was fondly remembered by many local people), Chung Mow of Hangkow ('the comic Tartar rebel dwarf') and the Peckham Giant Baby (a boy who, by Edwardian standards, was immensely fat). A strange stuffed kitten with two bodies and one head was grotesquely displayed in a jar.

Actors and literary figures also had a place on this floor, including Sir Henry Irving, Miss Ellen Terry and William Shakespeare. Also in this room was a small stage on which, according to the catalogue, 'all Freaks and Novelties' gave their performances 'at regular intervals'. One of the 'freaks' advertised was Miss Lucy Moore, 'the heaviest lady in the world': 'Miss Moore has been several times on view at this establishment, and is a great favourite with the patrons. Since the above drawing was made, Miss Moore's weight has increased by over six stones. Her exact weight during her first engagement here was 46st. 12lb. Unlike most ladies of abnormal avoirdupois, Miss Moore enjoys perfect health.'

After enjoying all that this floor offered, it was time to head up to the second floor. On the way up, paintings claiming to be 'Valuable old oil-painted panels by Van Dyke, valued at £500' hung on the walls alongside pictures entitled 'The Forsaken Beauty', 'Scenes in Japan', 'The

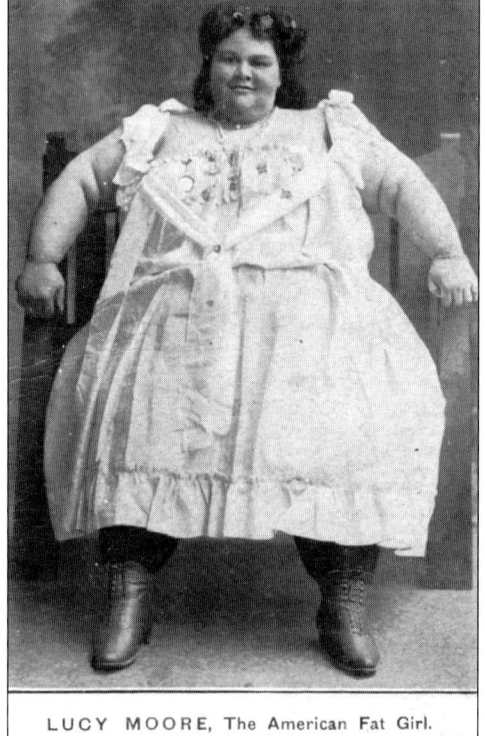

LUCY MOORE, The American Fat Girl.
Weight 46st.
THE RECORD FAT GIRL—STILL GROWING.

Lucy Moore

Punishment of the Wicked' and 'The Calling of the Righteous', as well as a collection of photographs of the various 'freaks' who had performed and been exhibited by Pickard in previous years. After this stairway gallery, the second room was entered, and here a whole new galaxy of delights was in store.

The visitor was greeted by waxworks of Pope Pius X and Margaret Scott, a lady who achieved the grand old age of 125 years. Cleopatra, Queen of Egypt, gazed alluringly from her perch beside the famous Glasgow grocer Thomas Lipton. There were also parisian models in wax, various paintings of animals being hunted and the enigmatically entitled 'Cosmoramic and Stereoscopic Art Gallery', but most strange of all was Sleeping Beauty, who was displayed lying in her bed throughout the day. The description of this lady is so remarkable it is worth including it in full:

THE SLEEPING BEAUTY – MADAME ST. AMARANTHE. A moving figure of a young lady of surpassing loveliness, in elegant repose, her chest and respiratory organs in apparent health and vigour, and breathing precisely as if alive. Madame St. Amaranthe, one of the most lovely women in France, was the widow of the lieutenant-colonel of the bodyguard of Louis XIV. Robespierre endeavoured to persuade her to become his mistress, but being virtuous as she was beautiful, she rejected his solicitations with indignation. Robespierre, who never wanted a pretext for destroying anyone who had offended him, brought Madame St. Amaranthe before the Revolutionary Tribunal, and at the age of 22 this victim of virtue was hurried into eternity.

Now, it is claimed by those who saw Sleeping Beauty that she was in fact a real woman and not a model. One lady remembers her father talking about this exhibit: when the sleeping princess needed to relieve herself, he said, she would very slightly lift the little finger on her right hand, which would alert an attendant of her need. The attendant would then temporarily pull a curtain around the scene, offering some excuse along the lines of the exhibit being in need of a clean.

After viewing this room, another floor waited above with more similar delights. Actually, this final room was the climax of the museum experience and was absolutely crammed to the rafters with goodies of every conceivable, and inconceivable, type: Zulu artefacts from the Transvaal War, three French automatons, a murderer's gallery displaying figures, portraits and short histories of Dr Edward William Pritchard, who poisoned both his wife and mother-in-law; Mrs Dyer, who ran a 'baby farm' and was accused of murdering one of the babies she had in her charge; Richard Davis, who murdered his father; J.A. Dickman; Samuel Herbert Dougall; Charles Peace; Edgar Owen (or Edwards) and the notorious Oscar Slater, a regular frequenter of the Glasgow music halls, who had been convicted of the murder of Marion Gilchrist, an elderly woman bludgeoned to death in her home in 1908. (In 1923, however, with the support of Sir Arthur Conan Doyle, Slater was to be acquitted on a technicality and released from prison.)

These exhibits were all squeezed in beside more educational items such as a 4,000-year-old Egyptian mummy (which Pickard claims to have purchased in Brussels at a cost of £373); a merman in a glass case; a Cherokee baby carrier, a piece of rope from the noose that hanged Charles Peace and the leftovers from that man's last breakfast; turtle shells; clogs from Holland and various weapons and armoury including flint-lock pistols and rifles, swords, sword sticks, daggers, African shields, spears, a bow and some poisoned arrows..

Throughout the room, as on the previous floors, the walls were adorned with the strangest collection of paintings and photographs. Between the various cabinets were a large number of mechanical and automatic machines and gaming machines.

Pickard's collection was auctioned off a few decades later, on 15 July 1935. He was interviewed at the time by a local journalist who quizzed him on the authenticity of some of the exhibits. When the journalist asked Pickard whether he believed his stuffed merman was indeed genuine, Pickard replied, 'To be quite candid, I think it was a piece of cod.'

Merman exhibited in Pickard's museum

The same reporter also spoke to Peter Pickard (one of A.E.'s sons), who gave away one of the great secrets of the execution exhibit. Executions were no longer viewed by the public and hadn't been since the middle of the 1860s. Deprived of this entertainment, they flocked instead to see model re-enactments of the hangings. However, because of the frequency of the executions, Pickard couldn't afford to create a new model every time. Instead, he would purchase the clothes of the criminal from the executioner and dress the existing dummy in them, re-labelling the exhibit with the name of the murderer of the day. Peter, however, assured the journalist that the model executions 'were even more popular than "The Naughty French Girl"'.

The journalist did not seem overly impressed by his experience of the museum, which he had managed to visit just prior to its closure:

> Crime has a large place in the museum and I found the exhibits infinitely more blood-curdling then those in the crime museum at Glasgow Central Police Station.
>
> One of the exhibits is the writing cabinet of Major Armstrong, the poisoner, containing a secret drawer in which he kept his poison. This cabinet was a production at the Old Bailey murder trial and Mr. Pickard made a special journey to England to buy it.
>
> On the way out Mr. Pickard threw open a wardrobe and revealed a body which might or might not, interest an anatomist. It was the embalmed body of Mary Bateman, a murderess hanged in Yorkshire. 'Notice how wonderfully it is preserved.' said Mr Pickard. But I was already on my way . . .

PICKARD'S WORLD-FAMED PANOPTICON

At the end of 1905, when Anderson was looking for a new manager for Britannia, it is very likely that the two neighbouring proprietors discussed the problem and that Pickard, not being one to see an opportunity go past, seized his chance. Anderson obviously saw some potential in this young Englishman, and in 1906 Pickard moved in to his new office in the 'Old Brit'.

Pickard was well aware of the building's problems: the lack of modern facilities (the ladies apparently still didn't have a loo); the wooden pew seating; the Victorian fixtures and fittings – its nickname, the Old Brit, was apt to say the least. Generally, any new manager would set about improving these conditions, but not A.E. He decided that he would rather invest his money on widening the variety of entertainments Britannia had to offer.

He had only been in the building for a few weeks when fortune smiled upon his idea. Macleod's Waxworks and Museum at 155 Trongate, was closing. Mr Macleod had recently died and his children, not interested in running it themselves, decided to sell the whole collection that their father had spent years accumulating. The auction was well advertised in the *Evening Times* and other local newspapers, which also commemorated the museum that had been 'one of the great Glasgow institutions' for over a quarter of a century.

Some of the items advertised as being for sale included wax figures of famous criminals, a 'quantity' of curiosities and historical relics, a number of stucco busts, some sculptures and several animals, 'both alive and stuffed.' The most valuable item was a device called a military orchestrion, which had originally cost £2,000, it was said to be the finest instrument of its kind in Scotland, 'giving the full effect of a military band of 40 performers'. A Russian sleigh, a height-and-weight machine used for many years in the Duke Street Prison, a model crank overhead engine, a 'serpentclyde or bass horn', a very fine French carved gilt suite from the Hamilton Palace collection, six fine old ecclesiastical armchairs with gothic backs, and a stucco figure of Sir William Wallace.

This sale afforded Pickard the perfect opportunity to acquire some new exhibits for his latest attraction in the attic of Britannia Music Hall. Rather than leave the way open for another competitor, it would appear that he bought the lot, including the animals, both alive and stuffed. However, the Britannia's attic was too small to accommodate several floors' worth of novelties, so he moved the gaming machines and some other novelties out of his neighbouring American Museum and into the attic of Britannia, in order to make room for the newly acquired collection.

For a few months, Britannia was again closed as Pickard worked away painting, building and adding many new fixtures and fittings, including a glazed roof area in the attic. Huge potted plants, strange packages and even stranger characters appeared daily in the Trongate, running up and down the stairs of the old Victorian palace of variety. The public waited with great anticipation to see what the new impresario would reveal.

In May 1906, Pickard reopened the building under the new name Britannia and Grand Panopticon. It was an instant success.

Under New Management
POPULAR AMUSEMENTS

By the opening under new management of the Britannia and Grand Panopticon, Trongate, yesterday a notable addition was made to the number of places of amusement in Glasgow. So far as the city or Scotland is concerned, it will inaugurate a new departure in respect that no fewer than six stage performances will be given daily, the first at one o'clock and the last at half past nine. Apart from the variety entertainment, people will find plenty of attractions in the building. There are various tableaux in wax, these including a representation of a torture chamber of the middle ages, the story of a Paris Crime, and Human Sacrifices in Dahomey. In addition there are various mechanical and automatic machines, an electric rifle-shooting machine, and many paintings and statues.

When Pickard had arrived in Glasgow, the role of proprietor was one that involved high drama and great showmanship. With lots of music halls, theatres and other amusements for people to choose from, each place of entertainment had to compete furiously with the others in order to secure the public's attention. Whilst the newspaper had become the regular publicity tool of the theatre manager, none had used this device as effectively as Pickard would.

At first Pickard used the same line as all his competitors, simply listing all the entertainments on view in his establishments, highlighting the biggest names and boasting the best novelties, but he very quickly cottoned on to the idea of including himself in the publicity, using a touch of humour to attract the reader's attention. His witty adverts in the local press stood out amongst the standard listings for competing houses. For example, many of the music-hall proprietors would end their advertisements with something like 'Sole Proprietor . . . Joe Bloggs Ltd'.

A.E. Pickard 'Unlimited'

After becoming the manager of Britannia, he took to doing the same. However, he would add a bit of humour to the caption by inventing comical descriptions of himself. At first he would end all of his adverts 'Sole Proprietor . . . A.E. Pickard Unlimited'. But before long he lengthened it to 'Sole Proprietor . . . A.E. Pickard Unlimited of London, Paris, Moscow and Bannockburn'. Not all his adverts made this claim as he was, of course, charged by the word. Realising that his humorous approach was already appealing to his public, he gave himself shorter, sometimes vain, but usually daft titles, replacing 'sole proprietor' with terms like 'King of the Trongate . . . A.E. Pickard Unlimited' or 'The Irresponsible . . . A.E. Pickard Unlimited'.

With all the publicity surrounding Pickard and the reopening of the Britannia, people flooded back through the doors of the music hall, and it was just like the old days as the hoards queued down the Trongate. The new name, Britannia and Grand Panopticon, however, was not as instantly successful. No one knew how to pronounce it, children in particular having great difficulty getting their tongues around the word 'Panopticon' and the building soon became known by the public as the 'Pots and Pans'.

But what is a panopticon? It refers to a type of prison which had gained some popularity in the 1800s with wardens because of its circular shape. The prisoners' cells were placed around the circumference of the circle and the officers observed from the centre, able to inspect every cell from one vantage point. However, the word itself comes from two Ancient Greek terms: *pan*, meaning 'everything' and *optikon*, meaning 'visible' or 'seen'. In Pickard's Panopticon, people could 'see everything' for the one ticket price, from the entertainment on the stage and screen to the entertainments in the attic. As Christmas approached, Pickard offered his audience even more to view when he advertised:

BRITANNIA

PANOPTICON

PICKARD'S FIRST ANNUAL

CARNIVAL

Will be held in the Panopticon

~

In addition to the CHRONOPHONE and

Grand Variety Company

Including

ALL THE FUN OF THE FAIR

Rifle Shooting, Cockernut Saloons, French Billiards,

Aunt Sallies, Pipe Breakers, Eliza Jones, Bogie Men,

Hookem, Love in a Tub, Ball Punchers, Weighing and Strength appliances,

And All The Latest

UP TO DATE AMUSEMENTS.

The admission price also included a visit next door to Pickard's American Museum and Waxworks, which could be entered via a connecting door behind the stage. (This door still exists today and it even still has a key in the lock. Sadly on the other side of the key hole, the door is bricked up.

NOAH'S ARK

By now it appeared that Pickard had achieved his ambition to create a palace of entertainments to rival Barnum's New York museum and London's Trocadero, but he had crammed so much into the two buildings, they were almost literally bursting at the seams. He needed to find more space and, beneath the pub on the ground floor (which by now was called the Hillcoat Bar), he found his solution. Pickard negotiated a price with the publican, Robert Hillcoat, and acquired the basement. Within days of settling the matter, he sent in the workmen and after many months of clearance, excavation and construction, it was ready to be opened. A notice appeared on 4 May 1908 describing the hall and its iron cages, 'strong enough to hold any kind of wild animal, bird or reptile', opposite which were a variety of pictures: 'coloured prints of Chinese tortures, rich engravings by W. Hogarth and other eminent artists, as well as some fine oil paintings'. There were also distorting mirrors and an organ, which would play 'some lovely selections' as the public was 'promenading round seeing the sights'. The notice continued:

Mr Pickard, who has been away on the continent, visited some of the leading European zoological gardens, including Paris, Berlin, Brussels and Antwerp, and secured some fine specimens of animals which are expected to arrive in Glasgow in the course of a day or so.

The opening of this novel 'Noah's Ark' will take place in the course of a few days, and it is gratifying to hear that Mr. Pickard has decided that no extra charge will be made to view this part of the Panopticon, so that all visitors and the usual Panopticon patrons will have access to this splendid collection. This is the first time that the title 'Noah's Ark' has been used to signify a collection of animals since the Biblical days of Noah.

Forty-two animal cages were crammed into the basement, and as the patron wandered between these cages staring in at the bear, monkeys, birds and reptiles on view, they must have been nearly suffocated by the smell. The audience in the auditorium two floors above complained bitterly about the pong, which indicates how bad it really was, able to overpower the noxious aromas of urine, tobacco, dirt, horse manure, sweat, and, of course, the smell of the first popular take-away food, whelks.

It must have been pretty tough on the poor animals too, who would occasionally make a bid for freedom. The bear had managed to escape from its cage and was seen tearing through the crowds and up the stairs to the rooftop carnival, where it climbed up the roof truss, through a hatch and onto the roof of the building. Pickard and some of his carnival workers managed to bring the bear down safely from the attic and reinstall it in its cage in the subterranean zoo. Soon after this first break for freedom, the bear escaped again, and this time it made its way straight out into the Trongate, where it proceeded to growl ferociously at passing shoppers. Pickard responded by turning the escape into a publicity stunt. He donned his plus-fours and, brandishing a huge blunderbuss, shot the bear in front of the assembled crowd of onlookers. After this tragic event, Pickard posted a notice: 'The bear . . . escaped from its cage at the Panopticon and was captured upon the roof of the building, it afterwards made another attempt to regain its liberty and became so ferocious that Mr. Pickard was obliged to shoot it.'

Another animal to make a bid for liberty was a golden eagle. Once again, this woeful tale made it into print in Pickard's catalogue: 'The Bird escaped from the Panopticon Zoological Collection and was run to earth at Alloa, after having been at liberty for nearly a week. The escape of this voracious creature caused considerable alarm among the inhabitants of the various towns and villages over which it was seen hovering; and Mr. Pickard himself heaved a sigh of relief when the tidings came from Alloa that it had been captured.'

Pickard, never being one to miss out on any publicity, not only promoted these great escapes, but even made his own short film entitled *Mr Pickard Goes Hunting*. Animals became a regular feature of Pickard's promotions, particularly the performing chimpanzees, who would be paraded around the streets advertising his places of amusement. Two of the chimpanzees, Solomon and his 'wife' Betsy, were relatively well-known performers in their day. Pickard billed them as 'Solomon and his wife; the missing links' and 'Solomon and his wife, the world famous educated chimpanzees'. Both were remarkably human in their behaviour, in particular, Solomon, who was never seen without clothes, and who always stood upright like a man when there was an audience of people to see him.

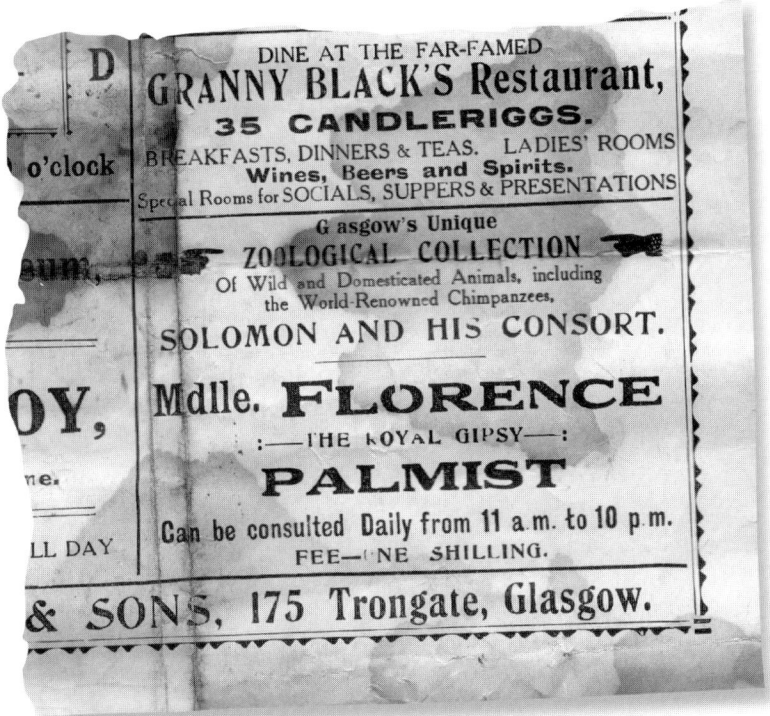

Advert for Solomon in a Panopticon programme

PICKARD THE PRANKSTER

By 1911 Pickard had become so confident with his local fame and that of his Panopticon (the new name he had bestowed upon Britannia) that he advertised a competition called 'Pickard's Titles':

> Mr Pickard offers two prizes of five shillings each and every week for public competition, one for the most humorous advertisement and the other for the funniest title. There is no entrance fee, and the only qualification attached to the competition is that all attempts must be written on picture postcards only. The competition closes on Friday morning each week, so competitors should see that their attempts are posted on Thursday evening at the very latest.

The response to this competition has provided us with a humorous insight into the public's opinion of Pickard and his Panopticon. Some entrants regarded the Panopticon and its proprietor as beneficial to general health:

> The Panopticon Pharmaceutical Phenomenon.
> Dispensary opens at 1pm daily.
> The sure cure for coughs, colds, sore feet, and torn clothes. Never known to fail!
> Treatment daily at 2, 4, 7 & 9pm by the following eminent specialists:–
> Brothers Fergusson, Fern & Wallace, Will Leslie, Daisy Scott, Karl Kroma.
> Testimonials from all the crowned heads, soft heads, bald heads, and stair heads of Partick, Govan, and Milngavie.
> Fee for course of treatment two pence
> Resident physician . . . A.E. Pickard Unlimited

Others regarded it as a flight to mysterious and exotic lands:

> Pickard's Panopticon.
> A trip to the 'stars'.
> Sensational flights to Zulu land, the happy land, Paddy's land and Paddy's Market. By the following aeronauts and aerosomethings. At 2, 4, 7, & 9pm daily.
> Aerodrome opens at 1pm fare twopence
> Notice:– for this trip ladies must have harem skirts and gentlemen must wear kilts made of leather.
> Lord of the smiles . . . A.E. Pickard Unlimited

Some entrants gave the building a much more dramatic billing:

PICKARD'S PANOPTICON
THE CELESTIAL CITY OF VALAHALA
The following host will twang their harps at 2, 4 ,7 & 9pm daily; The De Roney
& Wyman; Dolly Du Barrie etc; Wells & Flynn on the Bioscope Etc.
Doors open at 1pm Collection twopence. Enter, then ye proletariat, through
the pearly gates of the Panopticon and worship at the shrine of the immortal
Pickard the last of the great Hebrew prophets, and pain and sorrow shall be
no more.
The only way . . . A.E. Pickard Unlimited.

The titles the public sent in to describe Pickard ranged from appealing purely to the man's ego to showing how good he was at allowing himself to be lampooned. He even encouraged his public to provide him with slightly more insulting titles by goading them with the following notice in the papers:

Mr Pickard regrets to state that the attempts submitted in this competition during the last few weeks have, on the whole, been extremely poor, and there has been a marked deficiency in the really funny 'titles'. As genuine humour is one of the justly noted characteristics of the Scot, Mr. Pickard trusts that a little more of this evidently lately-latent quality be visible when choosing candidates for the next two cheques.

Amongst the little gems that resulted are: 'The Aberdonian spend thrift.', 'The smiling cod fish', 'Lord of the snails', 'The cock-eyed shrimp', 'The Knock Kneed Kipper' and 'The Skinless Sausage'.

The titles competition ensured that by the time he had been in Glasgow for a decade his name had become a part of the Glasgow vernacular. His infamy and self-promotion, however, went beyond the billings he and his public gave him in the papers; his very actions were to gain him notoriety beyond any other showman in Glasgow history. He could often be found sitting in the front row of the stalls in rival theatres, sometimes dressed in outrageous costumes and blowing bubbles through an old clay pipe, at other times heckling both the act and the audience, but generally creating some kind of diversion to distract and disrupt the entertainments on stage. Rival managers found Pickard's pranks a tiresome game and he generally ended up getting slung out, rather unceremoniously, onto the pavement.

His japes were also targeted at his own staff and audiences. In the foyer of the Panopticon, he displayed a sign which in large letters warned patrons to 'Mind the Step!' Plenty of people tripped over in anticipation of a step that wasn't actually there.

On another occasion Pickard had apparently called his secretary, Nina Barry, into his office. She duly arrived with notebook and pencil, ready to transcribe a letter. As she walked into the room, Pickard had his back to her as he had been placing a large ammunition shell on the mantelpiece. 'Look at this!' Pickard suddenly exclaimed. Nina looked up from her pad, expecting him to be showing off his latest acquisition, the shell. Instead he was standing in front of her with his trousers down at his ankles – an act for which today he would surely be arrested.

His pranks extended into his personal life, creating a catalogue of memorable moments over the years. He was, for example, the first man in Glasgow to receive a parking fine when he parked illegally in Central Station. He had booked tickets for an excursion to Rothesay by train, and he was running late. In his haste, he drove his car right on to the middle of the platform, switched off the engine and jumped into the nearest first-class carriage. When he returned to Glasgow the following day, his car was still parked on the platform, but a bit of paper – the city's first parking ticket – was stuck to the windscreen. The fine (just a couple of shillings) was at first ignored; after repeated reminders, which were also ignored, Pickard was eventually summoned to court, where he offered the judge a £100 note, a very rare item indeed. No doubt the court had to send out for change.

On a subsequent occasion, he was fined £30 or so for another offence. Again, he ignored the charge until he was summoned to court. This time, he arrived pushing a wheelbarrow which was filled with ha'pennies to pay the fine.

Money was one of the things that seemed to drive Pickard, and, whether it was because he had worked for it or not, he made a great deal of it and hated seeing it spent. Pickard's family still hold a cheque which is made out by Pickard to the Inland Revenue. The amount is for some £33,000 pounds. It is neatly written and signed, and is perfectly legal. However, on the reverse of the cheque, A.E. has written: 'The best of friends so easily parted.'

Showing off his wealth was a favourite occupation and he proudly boasted that he was a millionaire. He had eight cars, one for every day of the week and two for Sundays. One of his cars is remembered for its blacked out windows and a sign that read 'You can't see me but I can see you.' He was the first man in Glasgow to own a private aeroplane, and, when television first became available in Scotland, he had a huge television aerial put on the top of his Rolls Royce.

Pickard once parked a Rolls Royce in a field in the West End and offered it as a raffle prize. He sold thousands of tickets, people buying as many as they could for the best chance to win the expensive car, the cost of which was easily recovered in the process.

His extravagant purchases – and methods of dispensing with them – always drew attention, but it is as a property owner that he is best remembered. Cinemas, theatres and music halls only accounted for a small percentage of the property he owned all over Glasgow. He also had huge plots of land, tenement buildings and flats, townhouses, country mansions, shops, offices and even a few industrial buildings. At one time, it seemed that every street corner was adorned with the notice 'purchased by A.E.P. Unlimited'.

At one point he was reputed to have the largest portfolio of property in the city, other than that belonging to the Corporation (Glasgow City Council). Pickard used this fact once in an argument with a local councillor, when he exclaimed, 'You can't throw a stone in this city without hitting one of my buildings!' The councillor retorted, 'Aye, and if it hits it, it'll fa' doon.' For Pickard, it seems, was not the best at maintaining his properties.

Pickard returning from his travels, his car laden with his latest novelties

As a tenement owner, Pickard could be regarded as one of the original slum landlords. I was once told by a taxi driver that his grandmother had lived in a Pickard tenement flat from the end of the First World War until the end of the Second World War. She had been widowed with five children and Pickard's was the only accommodation she could afford, except that she couldn't really afford that either and never paid her landlord a penny in rent.

Pickard had too much of a social conscience to throw a widow and young children out onto the street. Instead, he never pursued her for the back rent, but nor did he maintain the building in which she lived. The taxi driver said that his mother used to tell him that every bucket, pot, dish and saucer was used in wet weather to catch the rain as it poured through the large holes in the roof.

On another occasion when Pickard was being interviewed, the reporter asked how much of Glasgow actually did belong to him, to which he exclaimed, 'Does Glasgow belong to me? Of course it does, when Fyffe began singing it belonged to him, I was going to take a court action out against him.' Pickard was referring to William Fyffe, who had become famous in the early part of the twentieth century for his song 'I Belong to Glasgow', during the chorus of which he sang, 'But when I get a couple of drinks on a Saturday, Glasgow belongs to me.'

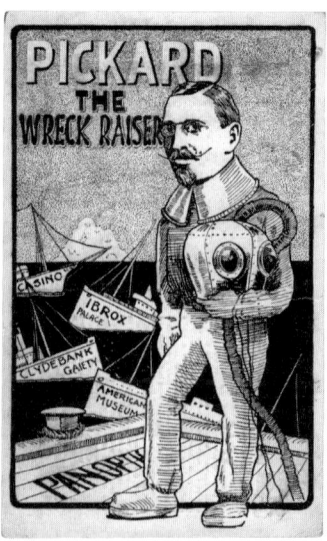

'Pickard the Wreck Raiser' postcard

Despite his great wealth, Pickard wasn't always generous to his family, however. Nina Barry remembered an occasion when his daughter called the office and asked for money: 'A.E. told me to tell her to go to the Parish like everyone else.'

His reputation for being tight with money was hinted at quite early on in his celebrated life as a Glasgow impresario and even featured in his own publicity. For example, a few years ago, we unearthed a small collection of torn postcards from beneath the balcony of the Panopticon.

It seems these cards had been torn up in disgust by the reader and when we pasted one back together and managed to decipher the text on the back we could wholly understand why.

The front of the card depicts A.E. Pickard standing dressed in an old-fashioned diving suit on a pontoon, upon which the name Panopticon is clearly written. Behind him is the river Clyde and in the Clyde are a small number of ships bearing the names *Gaiety, Ibrox Palace, American Museum* and *Casino* (which were the names of some of the buildings that Pickard had acquired just prior to the First World War). The card was entitled 'Pickard the Wreck Raiser' – probably because he was planning to resurrect the theatres sinking in the Clyde behind him, as he had done with the Britannia. But this is not what was causing insult to the erstwhile punter; it is what was written on the back that seems to have caused great annoyance:

THE MILLIONAIRE'S GRATITUDE
A Tale in One Spasm

He was well-dressed, from his glace kid boots to the crown of his glossy silk hat. As his sumptuously-appointed motor car drew up at the close in one of the slums he descended with plutocratic dignity, his movements disclosing the fur-lined interior of a coat which must have cost a king's ransom to purchase. Ascending one stair of the dingy tenement, he paused at a door and knocked gravely. A tired woman, looking half-starved and wholly dismal, answered. 'Do you know me?' inquired the wealthy visitor kindly. 'I dae not,' replied the woman. 'Well, madam,' said the million-man in a voice charged with an emotion he vainly endeavoured to conceal, 'I know you. Do you remember once giving a poor starving man a slice of bread and jam one cold, bitter evening many years ago. That generous meal saved the life of the recipient. He went abroad, prospered, until he is a millionaire. In short, I am that man, and I have called, not only to express my gratitude to you, but to present you with a token of my esteem for a simple act, which laid the foundation of all my fortune.' So saying the grateful millionaire dived into the interior of his fur-lined overcoat, produced a fat pocket book, and handing over a couple of cards, said – 'Here madam, are two passes for the Panopticon.'

14 MR A.E. PICKARD UNLIMITED
PROUDLY PRESENTS

IN THE ATTIC . . .

The animals of 'Noah's Ark' were only second in popularity to the wonderful assortment of people who could be seen in the attic space and adjoining museum. Here, bearded ladies, tiny men and human novelties of all conceivable kinds astounded the curious visitor.

This form of entertainment may seem repellent in today's times of political correctness and diversity, but, in the early twentieth century, seeing a different skin colour, dress or appearance was a novelty for many Glaswegians, and was therefore treated as one. People of all kinds were exhibited for profit in the 'freak shows', which have been hugely popular for centuries. In the Middle Ages, this entertainment was at its peak, as people flocked to see the oddities exhibited at the local fairs: tall people, short people, fat people, thin people, tattooed people, mer-people, hirsute

Princess Cristina

women, web-toed boys, conjoined twins . . . It was even rumoured that these shows were so popular, many of the exhibits were fabricated in order to keep up with demand. There are probably many cases where this is true: 'illustrated ladies', like the Panopticon's own Princess Cristina, would often have their tattoos painted on before every show. Victor Hugo, however, hinted at much more sinister practices carried out to satisfy the public's lust for novelty. In his novel, *The Man Who Laughs*, Hugo describes a most horrifying practice, in which a small child was placed into a porcelain vase with no lid or base. With just its head and legs poking out, the poor child was left to grow in the vase until its bones had moulded into the shape of the vessel, imprisoning the child. Unfortunately, I suspect that practices like this, and worse, occurred. After all, the freak show was one of the most popular forms of entertainment; people flocked to pay good money to see these exhibits and owners' fortunes were being made. Pickard was no exception – he would post notices boasting the number of visitors that his museum had received that week – 12,500 was a typical figure.

DIMINUTIVE PRODIGIES

General Tom Thumb, of Barnum fame, was the first-ever show-business millionaire. By the time Pickard opened his attic, however, he had been dead for several years, which meant that the name Tom Thumb became part of the public domain.

Pickard had his own Tom Thumb: a man who was, in fact, named Harold Pyott, and who was generally billed in other halls as Tiny Tim. Harold's height was described as being 23

Harold Pyott

inches, and he weighed only 24 pounds. He was born in Stockport on 25 September 1887 to parents of ordinary stature; his father was 5 feet 8 inches and his mother 5 feet 3 inches tall. Harold had two sisters, who were also of ordinary height, and were devoted to their little brother.

When Harold was only 12 years old, tragedy struck with the death of his parents. His uncle, Mr J.S. Beeley, took on the challenge of bringing up his nephew, who appeared to be in perfect health, apart from the fact that he wasn't growing at the normal rate. This began to concern his uncle, who consulted the local doctor. The doctor then sought the advice of some of the most eminent physicians in Europe, in an attempt to determine the reason for Harold's diminutive appearance. Harold was pronounced strong, healthy and of sound intelligence. He was, however, for his age, the smallest boy ever recorded at that time.

There was no record of illness to explain the boy's stature, but it seemed clear to Harold's uncle, and to Harold himself, that, as he was a full foot shorter than General Tom Thumb had been, he should become a performer and reap some of the rewards that his more famous predecessor had done.

Harold became widely known as Tiny Tim, until, in 1906, Pickard advertised the boy as Tom Thumb: 'Always on the outlook for novelty,' the *Evening Times* reported, 'Mr Pickard has made a hit with his engagement of Tom Thumb, "The most diminutive prodigy in existence."' Harold is further described as 'of cheery disposition, intelligent and speaks various languages. He enjoys perfect health and, although he has sailed the seas many a time, and has trouped through South Africa, France, Belgium, Germany and Ireland (twice), he has never been troubled with a day's serious illness.'

HAROLD PYOTT.   Aged 32 years, Height 23 inches, Weight 24 lbs.   THE ENGLISH MIDGET.

Postcard of Harold Pyott

Another small chap to cause a huge stir was the remarkable arrival of an actual Irish leprechaun! Pickard had heard it rumoured in 1908 that a leprechaun had been spotted by schoolchildren in Ireland. The children claimed that for days they had heard the tap-tap-tap of his miniscule hammer whilst he repaired his pots, and that, after following this sound, a group of the children had discovered a tiny man sitting naked beneath a huge dock leaf. A party was sent out to apprehend the little man and they captured him successfully. However, the little chap then seemed to disappear in a puff of smoke, as is the wont of fairy folk. The man was again captured shortly afterwards and was taken to the Mullingar workhouse where he was dressed in clothes and shoes which he instantly removed again. It was at this time that Pickard heard about the leprechaun from one of his agents in Dublin. He sent a representative to arrange a viewing to ensure that the leprechaun was genuine – far be it from Pickard to exhibit something bogus, of course.

After some negotiations, the leprechaun was procured by Pickard's agent and brought back to Glasgow to be exhibited. Pickard sent back the workhouse clothing and commissioned a local tailor to manufacture a fine suit of clothes of the highest quality, which the leprechaun duly refused to wear. It was stated in the *Showman* at the time: 'It will be a serious matter if it starts disrobing itself before the audience'.

The leprechaun, like Tom Thumb, could be viewed in both the Panopticon and Pickard's Museum, although most of the spectators were suspicious of the exhibit's legitimacy. The leprechaun was rude to the point of being foul, hurling abusive language at his visitors in between puffs on his corncob pipe, though he seems to have managed to keep his clothes on.

THE RETURN OF THE BEARDED LADY

In 1910 Pickard was to reintroduce to the Trongate audience what had once been a popular novelty: a bearded lady.

It was claimed that bearded ladies had not been seen since the days of P.T. Barnum some 25 years previously. Pickard played on this fact and promoted Maud Temple as his very own discovery, claiming that his agent had spotted her outside her own house in County Monaghan, Ireland.

Maud had suffered from an overgrowth of facial hair since she was 13 years old, and, as a result of the attention her beard attracted, she became a recluse and shunned society. In March 1910, Pickard managed to persuade the poor girl to be exhibited in the Panopticon and she agreed, after he offered her what is noted as a 'princely sum'. Once the engagement had been secured, her name appeared on much of the publicity for the Panopticon and the museum. In one article from the *World's Fair* newspaper, Maud was described as being 'of prepossessing appearance, intellectual, and most entertaining'.

Maude's hirsute appearance, it seems, was very enthusiastically received by Pickard's audience, prompting him to send her on a small tour around the world so others could see her with their own eyes.

Bearded ladies can still be found today at Coney Island, New York, alongside tattooed ladies, strongmen and the like.

THE UGLIEST WOMAN ON EARTH

There may still be some fascination for bearded ladies nowadays, but it's almost unthinkable to imagine an 'ugly woman' being promoted as a curiosity. However, in Pickard's time, a lady called Mary Ann Bevan made her living as one of the most successful 'ugly ladies' of Britain.

Mary Ann was born sometime in the 1870s in London to hard-working, honest parents. She was one of eight children, most of whom married early and left home. Mary Ann remained single and, after deciding that city life was not for her, sought a position in the country. She found herself a job as a farm worker, which she discovered quite suited her temperament and physical bearing – she was stronger and taller than most women (and men, come to that).

She never appeared to be remarkably different to anyone else and did not regard herself in any way as ugly – far from it: she was confident enough and not without suitors, and, when she moved to the country, she was quick to attract a husband.

By the end of their first year of marriage, Mary Ann was pregnant with the first of four children and it seemed that life was all she had hoped it would be. Sadly, as with all these tales, her fortune was about to change for the worse when her husband went off to fight in the Boer War.

Whilst her husband was away she took on much of his work with no complaint from the farmers who had employed him, but, when word arrived that her husband had died on the field of combat, the attitude towards her changed. The famers still wanted Mary Ann to work for them, but as she was no longer filling in for her husband, she could no longer command the man's wage. In those times, before moves towards female equality, women often found themselves doing the same job as men for far less money. Mary Ann decided instead to dress as a man, and secured herself work as a farm labourer in a neighbouring district where she wouldn't be recognised.

It was not difficult for Mary Ann to pull off this disguise as her plain features, height and masculine hands gave her employers little to suspect the true nature of her sex. She got paid very well for the work she did, until the truth was discovered and she was dismissed for her lie – after all, her employers argued, she was depriving a good working man of a job and income. The fact that Mary Ann had the same responsibilities as the working men was a protest met by deaf ears, so instead she returned home to her children and sought alternative employment as a domestic.

It was whilst working in service that she and a friend decided to take a day-trip to seaside. It was a welcome break from domestic chores and when they saw an advert for a beauty competition, Mary Ann's friend suggested they enter it, and they did.

According to Mary Ann's account, more people stared at her than at the girls who had made themselves up to look as pretty as they could. After awarding the prizes to the girls judged most beautiful, the organisers issued an extra prize to Mary for being the most un-beautiful. They also offered her a job, working in the travelling fairs and featuring in ugly competitions.

Mary Ann Bevan

In 1918 she entered a competition in London against 50 other entrants and won the first prize, confirming to Mary Ann that she was not average at all, but was in fact the ugliest woman in Britain. She didn't seem to be in the least upset by this; in fact she seems to think that it was very much to her advantage and a blessing in disguise.

As a result of her success, she had an offer to travel to America, and, since she had never imagined she would travel abroad, she took the chance and bought a passage on the Philadelphia. In New York she entered a competition at Barnum and Bailey's Circus at Madison Square.

The competition consisted of two prizes, one of $1,000 for the most beautiful woman and $500 dollars for the most unbeautiful. Mary beat 300 other competitors to win $500 and the dubious honour of the title 'Ugliest Woman on Earth'.

In the following couple of years, Mary Ann travelled across the globe to New Zealand, Australia, Africa and Europe, returning home in the early 1920s, when she managed to secure an engagement at the Panopticon.

PRINCESS IDA: 'THE HUMAN TRUNK'

Some of the people who performed or were exhibited had very apparent physical disadvantages that made them popular with the impoverished audience members, who only wished to gaze on those who were more physically wretched than they were. One of the most successful and poignant of these was Ida Campbell, 'The Human Trunk', who wrote of herself: 'born without legs and only one arm, I can knit, sew, crochet, and do all kinds of household work. I can work a sewing machine (hand and treadle), dress myself, do my own hair, walk about, get up and down stairs without the aid of crutches or sticks.' Ida's appearance fascinated visitors and she astounded them with her abilities, such as being able to thread a needle using her teeth and one arm. She could also produce the most perfect needlework using a sewing machine.

Ida had been born into a circus family in Chicago in 1874. Like many performers of her time, she produced a small biography which was published and sold. In this biography she attributes her physical disabilities to the shock her pregnant mother had watching the brutal mauling of her father, a lion tamer, by the lions in his charge. She describes how her mother had been watching her father rehearsing with his lions, when one of the

THE ORIGINAL HALF LADY
PICKARD'S MUSEUM GLASGOW

THE GREATEST LIVING CURIOSITY
To be seen only at PICKARD'S MUSEUM & WAXWORK, Trongate

Ida Campbell

larger males attacked him: 'the largest of the male lions pin[ned] him against the sides of their den; then there was a struggle for life between my father and the lion, but the beast overpowered him at the last, tore out his throat, and in less than ten minutes he was torn to pieces before his wife's eyes.'

Soon after this tragic event, Ida's mother was to suffer again when her son was crushed to death by a baby elephant. Soon afterwards, she gave birth to little Ida. The baby's abnormal appearance was the final straw and she died of a broken heart.

Ida was then put into the care of a Mr and Mrs Tollett, who were also travelling show-people, and, with them, she began her career touring and being exhibited in France, Germany, Italy, Spain, Holland and Russia. After this tour of Europe, they arrived in England, at which point Ida, who was very much allowed to make her own decisions, decided her fortunes would be better made with Bostock and Wombwell's Menagerie, with which she travelled across England, Ireland, Scotland and Wales. Ida's appearance was always guaranteed to attract a crowd. On one occasion, over 165,000 people turned out to see her.

Ida Campbell was typical of many of the people exhibited in these side shows. Doctors had no scientific understanding for the reasons of such birth defects and so would try and attribute it to some kind of trauma during pregnancy. Joseph Carey Merrick, also known as 'The Elephant Man', had a similar biography, which he travelled with and sold to horrified audiences.

In those times, if you couldn't work, you didn't eat or have a home, and many people like Ida, who were exhibited in such shows, had found themselves with two choices in life – either eke out an existence in one of the grim and prison-like institutions for the unfortunate and insane, or join a travelling show and be exhibited for money. World travel and a very healthy income – in Ida's case, up to £1,000 a week – were definite incentives to choose the latter option.

MONS BEAUTE: NIL BY MOUTH

Not all of the novelties on view, however, had been born with physical disabilities. One of the most popular of all was the one and only Mons Beaute, a man so popular that thousands of people queued for hours every day just to see him at his work. What were they waiting to gawp at? Why, Mons Beaute held the world record for fasting. Yes, people were queuing to see a man standing in a glass box, not eating. In those days, as I have already pointed out, times were hard, working hours were long and poorly remunerated, and it was difficult enough housing a family, let alone feeding them. To see a man voluntarily starving himself, and not losing any weight in the process, was therefore regarded as close to a miracle And Mons Beaute was exhibited for over 48 days.

Rumours spread that the fasting man had a hollow cane in which he kept protein pills, one of which he would pop into his mouth when no one was looking. Recent investigations have, however, unearthed the truth – the stage manager's wife would in fact deliver a steak pie to him after midnight, when the building was quiet.

Mons Beaute fasting in his booth

THE HUMAN SPIDER

Many of the novelties witnessed in the Panopticon were world-famed and are well recorded, but not all of them – it has been difficult at times to learn the true story behind some of the acts shown in the Panopticon. One of the most perplexing exhibits was 'The Human Spider'. A promotional postcard for this novelty, featuring an illustration of a lady, and signed 'A.E.P.' was found, and for several years we considered the possibilities that she was either a contortionist or had indeed been born with additional arms and legs. In one of her many hands, she is pictured holding what appears to

Advertisement for the Human Spider

be a cartoon representation of Sir Harry Lauder, whilst in another she seems to have Jack Buchanan in her grasp.

No other information seemed to be available, that is until we went to visit a gentleman in his nineties called Harry Hill. Harry had known the Panopticon throughout most of his early life, as his father and grandfather had been managers for Pickard. Harry had a stack of postcards portraying many of the acts who appeared at Pickard's Museum and Panopticon, but there was no sign of the Human Spider, so I showed Harry the copy of the postcard I had bought with me.

We didn't expect the reaction that followed as Harry burst into laughter. He giggled and guffawed until, gathering himself back together, and with tears of laughter rolling down his cheek, announced, 'It was my Aunt Flora!' Apparently Flora had been an usherette at the Panopticon and Pickard needed a volunteer to pretend to be a spider and eat rubber bugs all day. Flora got the job.

ON THE STAGE . . .

In the auditorium, Pickard always loved winding up the audience. He was notorious for becoming involved in the entertainments on stage, although not as part of the act. For example, on particularly raucous nights he could often be seen climbing a ladder in the wings, carrying with him a bucket, which he would hoist to the top of the ladder and then empty onto the audience below. The bucket would contain the rivets, nails and screws that the audience had previously thrown. He also taunted any act which was failing to gain the appreciation of the crowd by standing in the wings with a hook on the end of a pole. The audience would then encourage Pickard to use the instrument by shouting 'Bring on the hook', at which point he would drag the poor performer off the stage. This practice was a standard feature of the Friday amateur nights.

But for all his mischief, he continued to provide a bill of fare of which his predecessors would have been proud. The audience continued its reputation for boisterous behaviour; in fact it got worse, so Pickard began to employ juvenile acts – their childish, innocent ways proving an effective tranquiliser for the audience.

Babette and Raoul

THE JUVENILES

Babette the Wonder Child

One of the fabulous things about the juvenile acts is that some of them survived long enough to give me first-hand accounts of performing in the Panopticon, although sadly they have all now passed away. One lady, Betty McLauchlan, told me that at the age of eight she had been a frequent addition to the night's entertainment as 'Babette the Wonder Child'. A child performer who lived not far from the music hall, she would be taken from her bed, bundled up in blankets and put in the back of Mr Pickard's car. When she arrived at the Panopticon, she would be shoved into her costume and then pushed on to the stage to a chorus of 'Bring on the kid', as the audience, in characteristically riotous mood, pelted the comic turn on stage with rivets and rotten organic matter. Babette would then perform a routine of contortionism which would appease the baying rabble. Then she would be bundled into her blankets again and put in the back of the car, returning to her to her cosy slumber.

Babette the Wonder Child grew up to work as a professional with her husband Hugh McLauchlan. Billed as Babette and Raoul, they would perform a balletic routine, during which Babette would show off her abilities as a contortionist, famously taking on the role of a snake and sinuously winding herself around the body of Raoul, who played the part of her snake charmer. Babette and Raoul were also the first to use luminous paint in their act, which must have looked spectacular as the lights dimmed and all the audience could see were the mysteriously glowing patterns and lines as they moved.

Bijou and Bunty

Pickard was a sucker for a good sob story. One such tale came to me from Fay Lenore, who in Scotland was a famed principal boy in many a pantomime during her career, and leading lady in the *Five Past Eight* shows. She told me the tale of two child performers, one of whom was her mother, the other, her aunt.

These two little girls had started performing almost as soon as they could walk, busking for pennies on the streets of Edinburgh to help their parents pay the rent. They were skilled little dancers and their routines attracted the attention of one Lady Mansel, who at that time had a 'Juvenile Follies' troupe. Lady Mansel could see that these two girls had talent and so approached the duo's parents, offering them money for the girls and assuring them that the little ones would receive a good education and career in exchange. The parents were desperately poor and they must have felt that Lady Mansel could give their daughters far more than they could afford, so they accepted the payment of £50 per child and tearfully kissed their babies goodbye. That was the last the two little girls saw of their mother and father, who sold their daughters in good faith, though, unbeknownst to them, into what was effectively slavery.

The girls travelled the whole of the UK with Lady Mansel's Juvenile Follies, performing five or six shows daily. They danced for royalty and peasant alike in the music halls, theatres and concert halls, their little feet carrying them gracefully across the stage, charming every adult who saw them. However, the long hours of rehearsal, the hard floor of the stages and the lack of rest and inadequate nutrition meant these girls suffered hardships akin to the horrors of the poor-houses their parents had so desperately wanted to save them from.

On one occasion, the younger sister (Bijou, aged six), was having a difficult time learning a new step. She danced it again and again and Lady Mansel berated her for never getting it right. She tried and tried, again and again, Lady Mansel not letting her stop. For hours this went on until her feet had begun to bleed so badly with the effort that a trail of blood was following her across the stage. Bunty, the older sister, though only 12 years old, protested strongly at her poor little sister's ill-treatment, but Lady Mansel ignored the girl's petitions. In her frustration, Bunty head-butted Lady Mansel in the stomach, sending the lady into a furious rage. This resulted in poor Bunty being locked up on her own in the attic of the lodging house in which they had been staying. A day and night passed with no relief and only the most meagre rations of stale bread and water, so Bunty took her life in her hands and escaped by climbing out of the attic sky-light and shimmying down a drainpipe to the street below. She then walked all the way to Glasgow (which was a good few miles away) and headed for the Panopticon, where she had performed on a previous occasion. It was the only place in the city that she knew, and, as she remembered Pickard being a kindly man, she decided to petition him for a job. She stood with the other hopefuls queuing up to audition that day and when her chance came, she jumped on the stage and did a song-and-dance routine which cost the last of her energy. At the end of the number, she promptly fainted through exhaustion and lack of food and water.

Pickard took pity on the young girl and offered her a paying job as the juvenile lead and principle boy in that year's pantomime, *Morgianna and the Forty Thieves*. The show was a resounding success. Bunty worked as hard as she could to ensure that she always pleased the crowd and the young girl saved every penny she earned. Eventually, she had enough to return to Lady Mansel and buy back her sister. At the ages of six and twelve those two little girls took care of their own careers, and they performed successfully all over the country, billed as the Gordon Sisters, until they were in their thirties and married with little girls of their own.

It probably seems quite cruel that people treated their children in such a mercenary manner, but quite a lot of loving parents were forced to use their children's talents to keep a roof over their family's heads. Today, child performers are even more abundant, but modern legislation keeps them from the tortures that child entertainers formerly endured.

STAN LAUREL

Of all the youngsters that were paraded across the Panopticon's stage, Pickard was proud of one above all. This youngster was to become one of the most famous comics the world would ever know.

The boy in question was the son of Pickard's colleague and rival, A.J. Jefferson, another Englishman who had arrived in the city about the same time as Pickard himself.

A.J. and his wife Madge had had successful careers as performers in their own right, but once they started having children, A.J. decided a career as a manager would provide a more stable life for his wife and nippers. In 1904, after working in several English halls, he took over the management of the Scotia Music Hall, which at that time had become known as the Metropole.

A.J. was keen that his children should get a good education, something he himself had lacked as a boy. A good education, he felt, would lead to a stable job and a regular pay-cheque, but one of his sons, Arthur Stanley Jefferson – better known as Stan to his friends – had a different view. Stan thought that his skills in reading and writing were perfectly adequate by

Stan Jefferson in 1906

the age of 14 and so began playing truant from afternoon classes on a regular basis and spent the time at the Panopticon instead, sneaking in for the 2:30 matinée.

Here he would watch his favourite comics – people like W.F. Frame – and memorise not only the jokes, but also the facial expressions, costumes, body language and delivery. The Panopticon became his classroom, and he would return home and perform what he had learnt for his bedridden mother, Madge. She encouraged her son and Stan began to write his own routines, in which he would involve his school chums. Then, with a rehearsed sketch in mind, Stan approached A.E. Pickard and told him of his ambition to be a great comic. He was desperate to perform on the professional stage and begged Pickard for the opportunity to do so. Pickard asked why he wanted to be on stage and Stan replied, 'Because I'm funny!' So it was that a month after his sixteenth birthday in 1906, Stan got his chance to perform as one of the amateur acts on the Friday 'Go-As-You-Please' show at the Panopticon.

Stan approached his father and asked if he might have the night off from his duties helping in the Metropole as he wanted to finish his homework. How could a father refuse such a worthy excuse? He gave the boy the night off and Stan went home, but only to raid his father's wardrobe for a suitable costume and collect his routine.

It just so happens that the night of Stan's debut was a balmy summer evening and Stan's father A.J. had decided to take a short stroll and enjoy the weather. He had turned into the Trongate and was walking past the Panopticon when he saw A.E. Pickard standing at the front doors, also enjoying the evening sunshine. Pickard mistakenly thought A.J. was coming along to support his son's first ever public performance.

'You're just in time,' said A.E. to A.J. 'Your Stan's next on.'

'Ah, good,' said A.J. to A.E., not wanting to appear as if he didn't know what his son was up to. Together the two managers climbed the stairs to the stalls, where they found themselves comfortable accommodation in the orchestra chairs in the front row.

Stan bounded onto the stage in a comedy suit covered in patches and cut up at the legs to fit him in a comedy fashion. It took a moment, but A.J. soon recognised it as his best suit, and noticed that the lad was also wearing his best silk top-hat. Stan began his down-trodden spiv routine with a joke, which, legend has it, went something like this: 'I say, ladies and gentlemen, did you hear the one about the two butterflies? One butterfly said to the other, "Oh, I am bothered, I am bothered." "Why's that?" said his chum. "Because I couldn't go to the dance last week." "Why ever not?" asked the other butterfly. "Because it was a moth ball!"'

The joke received a response which, according to A.J., wasn't bad, although Stan remembered it quite differently, and is quoted as saying in later years, 'The act was bloody awful.' At the end of the joke, it appears that Stan had spotted his father sitting next to Pickard in the stalls, purple with fury, having recognised his sabotaged suit. Stan, now feeling a little nervous, decided it was time to make an exit and took off the hat for a final bow. But in his nervousness he fumbled and dropped the hat. He clumsily stepped forwards to pick it up, but his foot connected with it instead and he kicked it into the orchestra, where one helpful musician endeavoured to retrieve it, but tripped instead and trampled it. Stan's face was a combination of horror, fear and panic. The audience began to laugh. Stan, wishing that he had chosen a magic act instead, so he could disappear in a puff of smoke, began to side-step off the stage, grinning foolishly at the audience, unaware that the stage manager had already begun setting up for the next act, which was a trapeze routine. A hook left on the stage behind Stan caught on the back of his father's best silk frock coat and tore it clean up the back. Stan's face was a picture. The audience was sent into fits of hysterical laughter and Pickard himself wiped the tears of laughter from his eyes as he elbowed A.J. in the ribs, commending him on having a son with such consummate comic abilities.

A.J. could do nothing but agree that his son's face and natural physical comic ability (however inadvertent) was indeed very amusing and from then on he encouraged his boy in his pursuit of a life on the stage. He managed to get Stan an engagement with Levy and Cardwell, who were touring Britain with the pantomime *Sleeping Beauty*. Stan was given a role as a gollywog, who stood stock-still beside the baby's cradle – not exactly an opportunity to show off his comic buffoonery. Not long after *Sleeping Beauty* had finished its run, Stan was given the chance of a better role, playing a comedy character in the play *Alone in the World*. However, it wasn't until he joined Fred Carno's famous 'Mumming Birds' that he got a real opportunity to flaunt his skill.

Carno's troupe was at this time world-famous and always a box-office sell-out. Stan quickly found his feet. One of his first jobs was to understudy the lead, another young wannabe music-hall star by the name of Charles Spencer Chaplin. In 1910, the Mumming Birds, complete with Stan and Charlie, travelled on a cattle boat to America. Charlie and Stan shared rooms, and in one of his biographies, Stan described how Charlie would play the violin to hide the sound of sizzling when Stan was cooking. The two would then waft the resultant smoke and smells out of the window by furiously flapping their towels – cooking of course was not allowed.

America did not provide the instant success of which Stan had dreamed. They were to tour all across the country, but were only actually paid for the time they spent on the stage. The English company was used to touring Britain, where distances between engagments were short. The long journeys between venues in the USA, however, kept the performers poor. Stan gave up in Colorado Springs and, along with another performer, Arthur Dandoe, began the trip home. By the time they had reached Britain, Stan and Arthur had developed their own routine.

Back in Britain, the two lads tried their new act for a while before going their separate ways, Stan adopting a new partner, Ted Leo. Together Ted and Stan secured an engagement at the Royal Victoria Hall (the Old Vic), where their slapstick antics were a huge success. This led to the comedy duo being invited to join another troupe, Fun of the Tyrol, which was about to travel to Rotterdam. This was the beginning of a hard-going tour around Europe, which would end in every performer feeling the harsh gnawing of hunger. Finally Stan managed to gather enough money to head back to Britain and decided to try his luck again in the London halls.

Soon after his return, Fred Carno's troupe arrived back from their extended American engagement. Stan bumped into Carno's manager, Alf Reeves, whilst he was walking through Leicester Square one day. The friends began to discuss their recent adventures, Stan's tale ending in struggle. The Carno troupe, however, had managed not only to end on a successful note, but a return across the pond was already being planned. Stan, who was pretty much out of work at the time, didn't really relish the thought of another tour, but when Alf offered him a chance to rejoin the troupe, he couldn't resist. Once again, in 1913, Stan found himself bunking down with his old pal, Charlie.

In New York, Mack Sennett saw the Carno troupe and was particularly taken by the drunk routine provided by Chaplin. He immediately offered the young man a deal of $125 per week, and this gave Stan the chance to replace Chaplin as the comic lead. Sadly, Carno felt that Stan was too young to effectively carry off the drunken act, so his time as the lead was shortlived.

However, Stan then started his own troupe with two other young comics. He worked hard, writing sketches and developing comic routines which the trio performed in New York, Newark and finally in Los Angeles.

Stan had, for most of this time, billed himself at Stan Jefferson. One evening, however, he discovered his name contained 13 letters, and the superstitious lad attributed his lack of meteoric success to that very fact. He changed his name at that point to Stan Laurel, laurel leaves being attributed to victory. Funnily enough, in 1917, shortly after adding the name Laurel to his billing, Stan was approached to make a two-reel comedy film called *Nuts in May*. The script was written by Stan and director Bobby Williamson and the film is a simple comedy, featuring Stan playing a young man escaping from an insane asylum.

This film debut led to a one-year contract with Universal Studios, in which Stan played the comedy character Hickory Hiram: Stan Laurel had finally made the big time.

During the period that Stan was writing and performing in his own short films, another young man was beginning to gain the attention of the Hollywood studios, Oliver Norvall Hardy. As the decade turned, Hal Roach decided to cast Hardy as one of the characters in a film called *Slipping Wives*.

Stan wrote most of the gags for the film and also played a minor part alongside Roach's new find. Stan and Ollie stole the film and the rest, as they say, is history.

JACK BUCHANAN

Hollywood was to take many a young star from the music hall and immortalise them on the silver screen. Another debut act from the Panopticon, Jack Buchanan, was to become one of the first cinema matinée idols.

He was born in Helensburgh, only a few miles from Glasgow, in 1890, and was christened Walter John Buchanan, but everyone called him Jack. At school his best friend was a bright young boy by the name of John Logie Baird. John lived only a few yards from Jack and the two became inseparable. As boys, they rigged up a telephone system directly to each other's houses so that even when they were apart they could chat away to each other. Sadly, their friendship was cut short when Jack's father died suddenly. At this point, life for the Buchanans was thrown upside down. There was little in the way of pensions or savings and Mr Buchanan had left behind him some sizeable gambling debts. Jack's mother was forced to sell the Helensburgh house to pay the debts and she moved her family to Glasgow, where she rented a house large enough to take in lodgers.

Mrs Buchanan worked hard to keep her family in a comfortable manner. She had not been from a poor background and she had always had paid help to clean and cook. However, in her reduced circumstances, she was forced to clean her own house, opting to do certain chores, like cleaning the front step, under the cover of night so that her neighbours wouldn't see her.

Prompted by his family's predicament, Jack left school early and approached his father's old auctioneering firm for a job. Throughout his childhood, Jack had had an ability to make people laugh. He was charming, good-looking and oozing with personality, in short, an ideal candidate for the auctioneer's box. His father's old employer gave the lad a chance, as his father had been a very successful auctioneer, but sadly Jack did not have the quick eye and steely nerve necessary. He soon resigned from his position in order to pursue what he felt was the career for him, a life on the stage.

His first opportunity to perform came when he joined the Glasgow Amateur Operatic Society, where he quickly gained starring roles. Although he was still very young, his success with the society encouraged him to try for the professional stage. Aged just 21, Jack auditioned for Pickard, who, impressed by the young man's comedy and singing talents, offered him a week-long engagement at the Panopticon.

Jack took this first paid job very seriously and used what little money he had to travel to London, where he could buy some new material, a couple of comic songs and some vulgar patter, which he tried out on his girlfriend's father, who was a curate. He laughed heartily at the bluest bits and Jack began to feel confident about his forthcoming debut.

The day of his professional debut arrived and Jack must have felt quite a combination of excitement at the realisation of his dream and the sheer terror at the prospect of having to appease Glasgow's most notoriously harsh audience. He waited nervously in the wings until his name was called, then he stepped out onto the stage. He walked to the centre of the apron and began his patter with all the enthusiasm and gusto he could manage. The crowd received him with loud jeers, cheers and boos, a cacophony that didn't abate as Jack changed from patter to comic song. Jack tried to sing above the noise, but the audience increased its volume and Jack took it as a sign that the crowd hated him.

At the end of the number, having failed to raise his voice above that of the mob, he left the stage, fully expecting that his contract would be torn up. His disappointment must have been easily read by the stage manager who looked at Jack with amusement. 'I wouldn't let them catch you at that song again,' he said.

Another performer who was waiting to go on turned to Jack and said, 'Just wait 'til you see what I get when I go on, and I'm top of the bill. At least nothing hit you.' Jack soldiered bravely on through his first week's contract. His billing on the front of the stage read 'New Act' which meant that every night the audience bayed for his fresh blood. However, he never received the horrendous pelting that many of his colleagues suffered on a nightly basis.

All week he thought about his next engagement in Edinburgh. Civilisation at last! Well, the next week he stepped onto the stage of the Edinburgh Empire (now the Festival Theatre) and was greeted with silence. He began his act. Silence. He finished his act. Silence. This second week-long engagement was as torturous as the first, but at least in the Panopticon Jack had known his audience was alive, if nothing else.

Not long after his first forays on the professional stage, Jack, his sister and his mother moved to Brixton in south London. After three months, Jack managed to get a part in a production at the Apollo Theatre. He was paid a pittance for 13 weeks' work and at the end of it, found himself unemployed again. Unable to find any more work, he spent as much time as he could afford visiting the theatres and trying to learn what he could watching the more successful acts. He was very fond of the black-faced singer Eugene Stratton, famed for his song 'Lily of Laguna'. Stratton was one of the most popular variety performers of his day and Jack studied him, and his dance moves.

Jack began to teach himself how to dance and discovered he had a natural flare for it, so he began to include some of these new moves in his act and, after a bit of rehearsal, auditioned for the Camberwell Empire. His audition landed him with a contract which turned out to be as unsuccessful as his Panopticon debut – this time, however, he was engaged for three weeks. He was always nervous before going on to face a music-hall audience, a crowd which could smell fear on the new performers. Who could blame him? It was perhaps a good thing for Jack that his engagement at the Camberwell Empire was terminated after just one week.

Signed photograph of Jack Buchanan

In April 1913 he got a job in the chorus of the revue show *All the Winners* at the Empire, Leicester Square. In addition to performing in the chorus, Jack was also given the task of understudying two of the principal parts. One of the actors he understudied was Nosmo King, who had given himself this title so that his name would be up in lights when the 'No Smoking' sign was on. Jack was also to understudy Vernon Watson, who became ill one night and unable to perform; Jack jumped in, his nerves under control, and was a sensation. When word got back to Vernon of his understudy's triumph, he made a miraculous recovery and returned to work, fearful that his job might permanently be given to the new boy. Jack's first taste of success was cut short.

The two-month run of *All the Winners* heartened Jack, but it was six months before he would get his next chance to perform, this time dancing in a pantomime in the Theatre Royal, Birmingham. When this run finished he returned to London where in March 1914 he managed to secure himself another short contract back at the Empire, Leicester Square. This time it was not so much of an endurance test, and, seasoned from his earlier forays, he found himself fourth on the bill. It seemed that life was finally looking up, until one fateful morning in August 1914 when war was declared.

Men from all backgrounds were enlisted, and Jack did his duty by trying to sign up. However, he suffered from a weak chest which meant he was physically unfit for active service. So he remained in London, where suddenly the competition for male leads had thinned out.

In 1915 his fame really began to grow when he appeared in the long-running and highly successful play *Tonight's the Night*. Stardom wasn't all that 1915 brought to his door. Whilst staying with friends, Jack met and fell in love with a Bulgarian opera singer, Drageva. Drageva was described as being a great beauty, and, after a few months of wooing, the pair got married. They seemed so in love, and when they appeared in public together, people would declare what a handsome couple they made, but unhappily the marriage was short-lived. After a few months, their various work obligations meant the couple were touring with different shows. As their communications became less and less frequent, it seems the spark of their love fizzled out, and eventually Drageva disappeared altogether. They divorced soon afterwards, and, although it was never discussed by Jack, many of his friends at the time believed that the Bulgarian diva had used Jack in order to acquire British citizenship.

In 1917, he appeared in his first film, the British-made *Auld Lang Syne*. However, it was his stage work that really made Jack come alive as an actor, and it is this that he enjoyed most until the early talkies arrived. The talkies bought new opportunities, especially for actors like Jack, who had British accents and were able to sing and dance, as musicals were hugely popular for this new medium. Jack arrived in Hollywood in 1929 and appeared in films with Jeanette MacDonald, Fred Astaire and Cyd Charisse, becoming best known for the films *Bulldog Drummond's Third Round*, *The Show of Shows*, *Monte Carlo* and *Band Wagon*.

His Hollywood success notwithstanding, Jack still enjoyed the thrill of the live stage and even built his own theatre, the Leicester Square Theatre, which he opened in 1930. By this time he was a household name and the first real pin-up for housewives everywhere.

Jack died of cancer in 1957, shortly after he had returned to Scotland to open the new Scottish Television Studios in Glasgow.

THE LAST BOUT

The Panopticon was the site of a final public performance: in January 1910, Jem Mace, 'The Hero of One Hundred Fights', demonstrated his skills for the last time.

Jem was born in Norfolk in 1831 and was the last boxer to hold the English Heavyweight title under London Prize Ring rules. His Romany ancestry earned him the nickname 'Gypsy', whilst his fists would earn him the title 'The Father of Modern Boxing'.

In the professional ring he won 25 matches, lost 4 and drew 5, with no knockouts recorded, gaining him both national- and world-champion status on several occasions. In short, Jem was one of the most famous sportsmen of his era and he endeavoured to use his fame to improve the art of pugilism. He always promoted the use of gloves and, even though he had gained his reputation as a bare-knuckle fighter, he warned against the perils of this kind of fighting, and also enthusiastically promoted the new Marquis of Queensbury rules.

Prize boxing was not the lucrative sport that it is today, so in the Victorian era many prize fighters had a second career as exhibition boxers, where they would travel around to various music halls, circuses and shows and demonstrate their skills, offering men in the audience an opportunity to survive a round or two in the ring. Mace took this idea of showmanship a great deal further when he founded his own travelling circus, complete with wagons, tents, side shows and performers, his own act being the major draw.

In 1890, he fought his last professional bout for the British Heavyweight title against the Glaswegian champion Charlie Mitchell. Mace lost and, aged 59, decided not to make another attempt to win back his title; instead he gained a new one, 'Old Jem'.

During his long career as a prize fighter, he had triumphed over many of the great men of the day, including Sam Hurst, Tom King, T. Allan and Coburn. By the time he came to the Panopticon, he was well into his seventies, but still appeared a hale and hearty figure of a man. He arrived with his troupe of lady athletes and gentlemen boxers, and, as he emerged from the wings, the Panopticon audience roared their appreciation.

'On Friday night the Panopticon eclipsed anything that has ever been seen on any stage,' reported the *World's Fair*:

> Mr Pickard having been informed that Jem Mace was a master musician on the violin in his younger days, requested him to oblige the audience with a selection on the Friday evening, to which the old veteran readily assented . . . the house was packed long before the appointed hour, and hundreds were unable to gain admission. Further, Mr. Pickard had another surprise to give his patrons. He had arranged with the champion all round athlete of the world – another old veteran – namely, Donald Dinnie, to meet Jem Mace on the Panopticon stage, and here we saw the two old champions shaking hands before an enthusiastic audience. Cheer upon cheer rose as these two heroes clasped each others' hands. Jem then took up the violin and played Auld Lang Syne, the two veterans being surrounded by the various artistes, as well as his own troupe, the stage manager, and stage hands.

Following this display of camaraderie, Pickard took to the stage and gave a short speech in which he stated that 'it was an occasion which might never arise again to see two of the oldest veterans of the sporting world on the stage together'. Pickard also added that he would have loved to re-engage Mace and his troupe at the Panopticon for another week, but he had already engaged them for the Clydebank Gaiety, another one of his entertainment venues, and, as the bills were already out, he could not very well disappoint the audience there. Pickard concluded his speech by announcing that he felt such a momentous occasion should not pass without showing his appreciation. So saying, he presented each of the old champions with a gold medal. The crowd went mad.

Jem Mace died in November of 1910 and was one of the last of many to represent the skills of the fighter on Britannia's stage.

'SMASH, LADIES, SMASH!'

This next turn was not a fighter in the fisticuffs sense of the word, but rather a fighter for moral decency. Her name was Carrie Nation, and she was known across the globe as the 'Saloon Smasher'. Her fight was for the abolition of alcohol at a time when alcohol was the ruin of the age. 'Smash, ladies, smash!' was her battle-cry.

Carrie Nation, the Saloon Smasher, held a public meeting at the Panopticon in December 1908 to warn Glaswegians of the evils of drink. Underneath Britannia's balcony floor we have uncovered blank Temperance pledges dropped by members of the audience, which we believe are remnants of her 1908 visit.

Carrie was born on 25 November 1846 in Gerard County, Kentucky. Her childhood was quite normal, and, when she left school, she trained to be a teacher. This was not a successful avenue for Carrie, who found her temperament constantly being challenged by her pupils, so when she married in 1867, she gave up teaching to become a good wife and, hopefully in time, a mother too. Her first husband was Dr Charles Gloyd, a physician, and together they had one daughter, Charlene.

Gloyd was an alcoholic and his excessive drinking kept his wife and daughter poor. When Charlene became sick and died in infancy, Carrie blamed her husband's excessive drinking. Unable to reconcile her feelings about her husband's alcoholism, Carrie's marriage was not to last, and within a year she had left her husband.

Ten years later she remarried, this time setting her sights on a man 19 years her senior who was also a well-respected pillar of the community; he was David Nation, a minister. Under his influence, Carrie became a devout woman and, through her dedication to scripture and to God, her calling became clear: she must lead the war against the vices of tobacco and liquor.

In 1880 the voters of Kansas adopted a constitutional amendment, prohibiting the manufacture of intoxicating beverages, except for medicinal purposes. Kansas saloon-keepers, however, did not adhere to the law, and neither did a large section of the male population. Carrie asked God to use her to save Kansas and God told her to go to Kiowa, a town in Kansas, which she did, and there she smashed her first saloon on 1 June 1900. It was the start of her career.

Soon people from other counties urged Carrie to save their towns from saloons. She promptly obliged, using stones and bricks wrapped in newspaper, but before long she purchased herself the small hatchet for which she would become famed. The hatchet became a symbol of her mission and pewter hatchet brooches went on sale, her thousands of supporters buying the brooches to show their support. The resulting income paid Carrie's numerous jail fines; between 1900 and 1910, the pious lady was jailed 30 times!

Even Carrie's enemies were compelled to acknowledge that her extraordinary methods had produced definite and concrete results. In less than six months, she did more to enforce prohibition laws than had been done by churches and Temperance organisations in the years before or since.

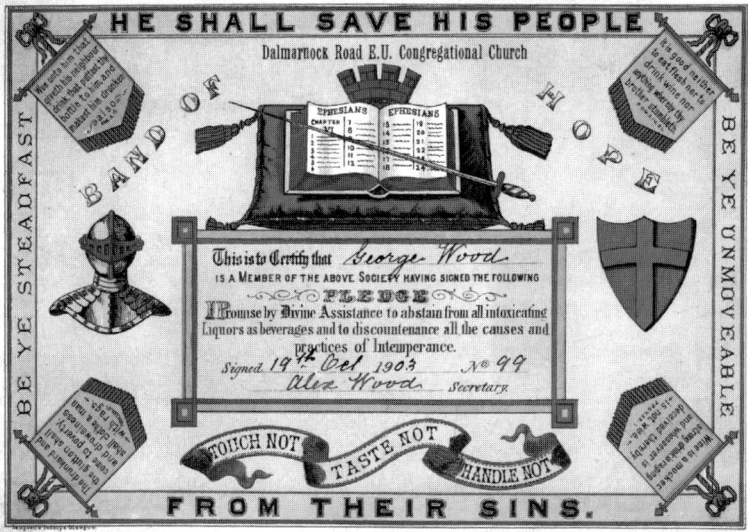

Temperance pledge from 1903, similar to those found in the Britannia Panopticon

Standing nearly six feet tall and weighing 180 pounds, Carrie Nation was a lady not to be meddled with. As a member of the Women's Christian Temperance Movement, she had been jailed on numerous occasions for entering saloons in the United States and smashing all the bottles of alcohol with a hatchet! No one stood in her way; even the prize fighter John L. Sullivan was reported to have run and hid when Nation burst into his New York City saloon. From 1908 to 1909 she extended her crusade to Europe, and it was on this tour that she visited Glasgow. Her appearance at the Panopticon, according to the local press, was a last-minute decision of hers, prior to her departure for Aberdeen. Nonetheless, crowds began queuing from 4 p.m., hours before the show was advertised to begin, causing mayhem on the Trongate. Police were sent out to control the traffic and the swarms of people, and, when the doors to the Panopticon opened, many punters were turned away, much to their disappointment. An article from the *World's Fair* on 2 January 1909 describes the rest of the evening:

At seven o'clock sharp the sacred concert commenced, it wasn't until eight o'clock that Mrs Nation arrived in Mr Pickard's motor car, having been detained at the Primitive Methodist Church, Alexandria Parade where she had been lecturing that evening. Her arrival was signalled by cheers and hooting from the crowds outside, and some difficulty was experienced as the police tried to keep the crowds back, while the motor car was run up to the side entrance of the Panopticon. A few minutes later the sprightly old lady was on the platform, and here another ovation was in store for her. Carry [sic] bowed her acknowledgements and with a smile upon her face and a bible in her hand she addressed the crowded meeting, explaining how she started her crusade against drink, how she smashed the saloons in the States with her hatchet, and what induced her to visit her cousins on this side of the 'Herrin' pond'. She described her experience in Scotland, where she had seen women and children half clad and foodless, which were the results of that hellish curse drink. At the conclusion of her lecture she thanked Mr Pickard and the audience for the cordial welcome she had received, and hoped she might be spared a visit to the old 'Brit' again shortly. She left the mass outside, as she journeyed along to her hotel. We hear on good authority from some of the oldest inhabitants of the Trongate that this was the largest gathering ever witnessed in this part of the city.

On 9 June 1911, a few years after her appearance at the Panopticon, Carrie Nation died penniless in Levenworth, Kansas, where she is buried beside her mother. Her epitaph reads: 'She Hath Done What She Could'.

CARY GRANT

Archie Leach is rumoured to have performed in the Panopticon, and although no actual evidence survives, many people are convinced that the old music hall saw an early performance by the man better known as Cary Grant.

He was born in Bristol on 18 January 1904 and christened Archibald Alexander Leach, a name he was to keep until he moved to Hollywood, where, unsurprisingly the name was not regarded as quite right for a matinée idol. (Interestingly enough, however, the name Archie Leach did appear in several of his films, most notably in *Arsenic and Old Lace*, on a headstone in the graveyard, and in *His Girl Friday* when Cary comments, 'The last man who said that to me was Archie Leach, just a week before he cut his own throat.'

Archie's life did not begin in the happiest of ways. His mother, Elsie, was sent to a mental institution when he was only about 10 years old. She had suffered from serious bouts of depression since the death of her first son who had died in infancy and she never recovered from this tragedy. One day when Archie returned home from scouts, his mother had gone. His father explained that she had gone into hospital for a while because she was very tired.

Young Archie was a bright lad and worked hard at school, winning a scholarship to Fairfield Grammar. By the age of 14, he had had enough of school and did everything to get expelled, finally succeeding when he was caught hanging out in the girls' toilets. Freed from his educational obligations, Archie ran away from home and joined the Bob Pender Troupe. He convinced Mr Pender (a wonderful physical comedian and acrobat of his day) that he was 16 years old and Mr Pender, who was finding it difficult to get young men due to the war, gave the lad a chance, but it wasn't long before Archie's father found him and took him back home.

A year later, his father gave him permission to rejoin the troupe and Archie worked hard to be the best acrobat he could, Mr Pender proving to be a magnificent and patient teacher. Archie didn't just learn about stilt-walking and tumbling: Mr Pender insured that his boys got a good grounding in other areas, and Archie was taught about scenic painting and stage management as well.

As his act improved, he and two others in the troupe founded their own little troupe as an amateur act. The pay was pretty poor with Pender, so, when the boys were performing at their paid job, they would check the local papers to see if any of the music halls in the area were offering an amateur competition with a cash prize. In 1919, the Bob Pender Troupe had been engaged to play at the Glasgow Pavilion. The house was full. Backstage, Archie and his pals scanned the evening papers in search of the opportunity for a bonus and found one. Where was the cash prize available that Friday? Why, none other than the Panopticon. According to a lady I met, whose father had performed with Archie, he and his friends performed at the Panopticon, and their act surpassed any of the others that night. The prize was easily won by the trio.

Soon after this triumph at the Panopticon amateur night, Bob Pender secured a two-year tour of America. In 1920 he packed up eight of his best lads (one of whom was young Archie) and sailed to the States on the same liner as Douglas Fairbanks, who was returning home with his new bride, Mary Pickford. Archie even managed to be photographed with the newly-weds.

Upon arriving in New York, Archie became ill with rheumatic fever and spent the first six weeks of the tour in bed. Once he was well again, he joined his colleagues on stage. The two years spent touring were a great success. Although the troupe returned to Britain in 1922, Archie stayed behind, sensing the world of opportunity that awaited him, although, as it turned out, this was not quick in coming. In order to survive, he earned money by turning his hand to various jobs, including cashing in on his acrobatic skills: from the top of his stilts, he promoted Broadway shows, using a megaphone to reach the ears of public below.

After five years of auditions, shows, minor roles, and working whenever and at whatever he could (including a stint as a male escort), he got his first decent role in the Broadway show *Golden Dawn*. His performance was a success, and his handsome looks and British accent lead him to appear in a number of Broadway musicals before landing his first (uncredited) Hollywood film role in 1931, playing a sailor in the 10-minute short *Singapore Sue*. In his next film, *This is the Night* (1932), he appeared in the credits as Cary Grant; his long and illustrious Hollywood film career had begun.

15 THE FINAL YEARS

Whatever the act, exhibit or audience, the Panopticon continued to thrive into the 1920s, with three or four shows daily. But as cinema began to take the place of music hall, the auditorium gradually became emptier. The novelties in the attic ceased to draw the crowds, and the basement zoo, with its now depleted stock, was finally closed. Pickard continued to add more to the bill and even closed the Panopticon down in order to achieve what he advertised as some radical changes in the building, including a new Art Deco auditorium and all the latest technology. It reopened in 1924 with the new title, Tron Cinema (although this soon reverted to Panopticon) but that was all that was new, other than a lick of paint to approximate the fashionable Art Deco interiors of the day. The wooden benches still creaked beneath the audiences' weight and the facilities were still Victorian and inadequate (although the ladies did by now have a W.C.). In short, the auditorium was largely unchanged from the music hall of earlier years, and seen by many as a bit of an old flea pit.

Pickard no longer promoted the building with the same humorous ferocity he once had, although he did continue to apply his imaginative marketing practises to his other ventures: when he first opened the White Elephant cinema (latterly known simply as The Elephant), for example, Pickard advertised dinner and a fur coat, free with the one-shilling admission, to the first 2,000 people to enter the new cinema. Women flocked to the building in their thousands, queuing almost back to the city centre, desperate to win dinner and a fur coat. How disappointed they must have been when they finally got to the front of the queue to discover A.E. Pickard and the cinema manager standing at the front doors handing out rabbits.

One of Pickard's larger projects was the old Norwood, a former ballroom on Glasgow's St George's Road, which Pickard converted into a cinema with sumptuous furnishings, plush carpets and gleaming mirrors. This building became a landmark in Glasgow, best remembered for the large model of the Forth Rail Bridge which was located on the top of the

Pickard with a battering ram at the opening of the Norwood Cinema

canopy above the front doors. In the foyer, Pickard proudly displayed a Kilmarnock edition of the works of Robert Burns, which he had bought in auction at great expense, a fact he enthusiastically broadcast. Being ever the showman, the opening of the Norwood Cinema in 1936 was a newsworthy spectacle, with Pickard himself forcing open the doors using a huge battering ram.

However, the 1930s were hard times financially for many of Glasgow's citizens, and the number of cinema-goers dwindled as a result. Although many of the cinemas and music halls tried to attract punters by offering a special admission charge of only three 'jeellie [jam] jars', all places of amusement suffered. In the spring of 1938, the Panopticon was finally closed.

Pickard sold the building to his tailors, Weaver to Wearer. They also bought out both of the ground-floor units, which had once housed the pub, music-hall entrance and shop, and turned it into their flagship store for Scotland. The first floor of the auditorium once again became a warehouse and factory. The balcony was obscured and sealed away above a false ceiling supported by a large timber roof truss.

Hidden she may have been, but the grand old lady of the Trongate continued to serve the people of Glasgow. During the Second World War, Glasgow Corporation used vacant floors of buildings all over the city for the war effort. In the case of Britannia Panopticon, the balcony became a chicken farm, keeping the people of the East End supplied with fresh eggs and some of the iron railings from one of the staircases were removed to make munitions, although it turned out to be the wrong sort of iron. After the war, other than the odd employee tripping across the upper auditorium by mistake, or the occasional theatre fan who managed to gain a quick glimpse, the Britannia Panopticon Music Hall remained forgotten.

A.E. Pickard continued his life as a prominent, self-promoting Glasgow resident until his death in a fire at his home in 1964 at the grand old age of 90. His eccentric business management had left a legacy which was commemorated in a series of wonderful obituaries, the most touching of which simply stated, 'A man died in a house fire last night and a legend died with him, for that man was A.E. Pickard'.

Panopticon building after its conversion into
Weaver to Wearer

Staircase leading up to the carnival floor

16 BRITANNIA PANOPTICON TODAY

On that cold February day in 1997, after years of research into music hall and the building's history, I finally stepped through the door and saw the balcony by torch light for the first time. I felt the ghosts stir: the crowd vigorously singing along to 'Ta-Ra-Ra-Boum-De-Ay', the boys jeering from the balcony, Stan's first faltering gag; even the smell of whelks seemed to linger faintly. The magic of the moment did not escape me, and I was filled with awe. Why had no one done anything about this building? How could this rare survivor of such an evocative era stay hidden above an amusement arcade, mouldering away?

'What are you going to do with the auditorium?' I asked the owner.

'Nothing,' he replied. 'I only brought the building because of the commercial space on the ground floor. I had no idea this was up here until the roof began to leak.'

'Has anyone else seen it recently?'

'No. An old woman who said she was Stan Laurel's daughter came last year and asked if she could get in. I told her the same as I told you, that there was nothing left worth seeing. Anyway, if you're so interested in it, why don't you do something about it?'

I laughed. 'What could I do? I'm a tour guide and a local-history buff, not a property developer – I wouldn't know where to begin.'

Suddenly someone shouted up the stairwell 'Phone!', and my visit to Britannia was over. I reluctantly followed the owner back out of the door, stealing a last gaze into the gloom before he closed it behind us. But I knew I would be back, and I hoped that I would get the chance to have a good look about and really soak up the ambience.

A couple of weeks later I again met Helen in the building, and this time I was allowed to wonder around the whole place with a good, strong torch. I dashed up the stairs and back through the door, but I couldn't see how to get beyond the roof truss and into the rest of the auditorium. There must be another way. I stepped back onto the half landing and followed the rest of the stair up to the top floor, where the door to the attic stood wide open.

I entered a cavernous space, brightly lit by the windows at the front that faced into the Trongate. The attic was a clutter of window-dressing props, mannequins, clothes rails, boxes of coat hangers and old display stands encrusted with pigeon droppings. Fragments of the once-grand carnival still survived, and bits of peeling pink wallpaper spattered with large daisies covered one wall. Behind one of the peeling lengths, someone had left their name, although all that could be discerned was the word 'Duettists' and the date, 1898. Scraps of the petition that separated a raised section of the attic into booths still clung to their timbers, as did the remnants of ornate plaster. These must have been the booths in which Tom Thumb, Ida Campbell, Maud Temple and all the others had been exhibited. I picked my way across a raised section (beneath which a gap allowed the ventilation of the auditorium below), very aware of the delicate nature of the floorboards, and went down three steps onto a floor which dipped alarmingly. This expanse of floor had once been the location of the wax exhibits and fairground amusements – the gaming and fortune-telling machines, 'cockernut' shies and electric rifle ranges. The whole area basked in the sunlight which streamed through the huge, arched windows.

Beneath these windows a staircase led down and I followed it to the balcony floor below. These stairs were a little unnerving to walk down as the iron railings that held up the banisters had gone (to the war effort), leaving a perilous drop along the edge of the stair. I had never seen the Trongate from this vantage point before, and, after I had recovered from a mild wave of vertigo, I took a good few moments to take in the view through the windows along the other side of the staircase.

At the bottom of the stairs, large double doors with the words 'Balcony Entrance' written across them lead me into the auditorium. I used my torch to find my way around the front of the old projection box (one of the only twentieth-century additions) and to a part of the balcony that was still fully seated. Using my sleeve to push away the decades of dust, I sat down with a feeling of satisfaction – I was probably the first person to sit on that old pew for 59 years. Then I began wondering about who the last person before me had been. I finally got up from my contemplation three hours later; my torch light had fizzled to a dull glimmer.

Somehow, just by occasionally visiting the building over the course of a few weeks, I got to know the girls working in the amusements arcade, as well as Mr Mitchell, who ran it, and the people who worked in the clothing warehouse on the first floor, where there had once been the stalls (in which A.J. Jefferson had sat with A.E. Pickard on the night of Stan Laurel's debut). None of the staff ever minded me being upstairs; in fact, we all became quite friendly.

By the end of the summer, I was leading a campaign to bring Britannia back to life, and other people were gradually starting to join in. Among the first was Graham Hunter, who has since become one of my dearest friends. He had worked in theatre and television for a number of years, designing costumes and sets, and his enthusiasm for the building and its history matched my own. In previous years, Graham and some of his friends had tried to gain support for the preservation of Britannia Music Hall, but without access to the building, the campaign had collapsed. Now, like me, he had the chance to help bring this old hall back into notoriety.

The building itself held many surprises: one day in October 1997, Graham asked me if I thought it would be alright for him to have a poke about the balcony. He said that he had rummaged around the old Athenaeum theatre after it had closed and found a few ticket stubs. 'You never know,' he said optimistically. 'I might find some treasure under there.' Well, he sure did. On his first journey under the balcony he came up with cigarette packets (mostly the little Will's Woodbines paper packs that held five cigarettes), some badly decayed, others almost perfect; whelk shells; a clay pipe stem; a couple of fly buttons and a few scraps of old paper, which, when cleaned up, turned out to be bon-bon wrappers.

I carefully wrapped each item in tissue and sealed them in little bags on which I wrote a reference number relating to where it was found.

Over the following months, Graham went under different areas of the balcony, beneath the projection room and under the floor of the rooftop carnival, sometimes on his own and sometimes with a couple of his pals. Every time they put their hands beneath floorboards or crawled into a gap, they came out with some new gem. The odd, well-preserved Woodbine pack no longer held the same delight – now they were pulling out whole newspapers from the 1920s, wax fingers and bits of wax face, baby rattles and teething rings, handkerchiefs, scraps of playbills and hundreds of tickets, even tickets for other venues such as the Star Palace in Bridgeton. They found hairpins, hatpins, flag pins, poppies from the first Remembrance Sundays, nappy pins, tie pins, sweetheart brooches, clay pipes, cheroot wrappers, sweetie bags, chocolate wrappers, bread wrappers, beer bottles, the lead seals from whisky bottles, colourful celluloid balls, rubber balls and marbles, bits of a broken peg doll, tram tickets (including two which were found rolled up together and clipped at the same place, perhaps dropped by a courting couple),

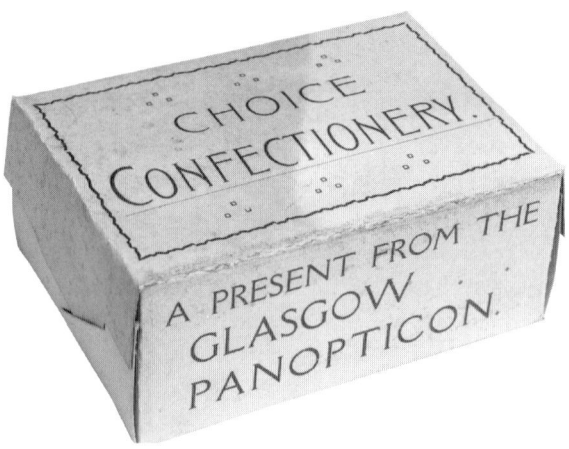

trade-union fliers, Temperance pledges, business cards, a Charlie Chaplin cane and the head from a Chaplin doll, a Pathescope badge, bits of film and pieces of a magic lantern slide, a glove, a cloche hat (brand new with no wear on the lining at all) and various bits of torn skirt-frill. Beneath the projection room, they found a glass eye, a collection of pools coupons, 30 or so Woodbine packs, an IOU to 'Nellie for 3s 4d', and five torn envelopes with 'Be My Valentine' written on them – conjures up quite a picture of the projectionist, doesn't it? Some other artefacts, though, were far more poignant, like a tiny brass ring with 'Baby' engraved on it and a wedding band made from an old penny – many people couldn't afford a gold band, so took a new penny to the shipyards where it would be pressed into a ring. This ring has been so carefully pressed that the date 1897 can still be seen inside. To whom did this ring belong? Does one of her grandchildren walk along the Trongate today?

All of these objects were fragments of the lives that once populated Britannia Music Hall. These were the ghosts.

Over the years, the interest in Britannia gained momentum. The story of the building began to appear in newspaper and magazine articles, as well as on the radio. In 1998, the first documentary about the building was made for Scottish Television by Beverley Morrison, who also got hooked on the story of this little building, then, in 2003, came the biggest publicity boost of all, when Britannia Panopticon featured in the BBC's new television series *Restoration*. As part of the filming agreement, we opened the doors to the general public for the first time in over 60 years. The Mitchell family, the owners of the arcade downstairs who have always been generous to a fault, had the false ceiling removed, and, in the summer of 2003, Britannia Panopticon rang again with the sounds of the music hall. Volunteers performed some of the old music-hall songs and Graham and I joined in; I played the juvenile lead, Florrie Bow Wow Bowers, and Graham took on the role of chairman, rivalling the great Leonard Sax.

Britannia didn't win *Restoration*, but we really don't mind; the publicity has been worth as much as a cash prize and today we open regularly for music-hall shows, Laurel and Hardy film nights, burlesque shows, exhibitions and, occasionally, more dramatic pieces, such as *The Whitechapel Murders*. It seems that new stars are to be found in Britannia Panopticon, with audiences once again cheering their approval.

A charitable trust has now been established to help with the fundraising and look after the future interest of Britannia Panopticon. In fact, at the time of writing this, the Britannia Panopticon Music Hall Trust is in the process of securing a long-term lease for the building. Subscribers to Friends of Britannia Panopticon and the Friends of Britannia Panopticon Charity Shop ensure that the campaign can afford to continue.

Meanwhile, I work in Pickard's former office. I can hear the sound of the modern city below, but am just a few steps away from the auditorium – my own Narnia – where the magic of the music-hall era lingers on.

SELECTED BIBLIOGRAPHY AND SUGGESTIONS FOR FURTHER READING

BOOKS

Baker, Richard Anthony, *British Music Hall: An Illustrated History* (Stroud: Sutton, 2005)

——, *Marie Lloyd: Queen of the Music Halls* (Bath: Chivers, 1991)

Barr, William W., *Glaswegiana* (Glasgow: Vista of Glasgow, 1973)

Bruce, Frank; Foley, Archie and Gillespie, George (eds), *Those Variety Days: Memories of Scottish Variety Theatre* (Edinburgh: Scottish Music Hall Society, 1997)

Drimmer, Frederick, *Very Special People* (London: Bantam, 1976)

Earl, John and Sell, Michael, *The Theatres Trust Guide to British Theatres*, 1750–1950 (London: A. & C. Black, 2000)

Eyre-Todd, George, *The Story of Glasgow* (Glasgow, London: 1911)

Fountain, Nigel, *Lost Empires: The Phenomenon of Theatres Past, Present and Future* (London: Cassell Illustrated, 2005)

Grant, Neil, *Laurel and Hardy* (Bristol: Parragon, 1994)

House, Jack, *Music Hall Memories* (Glasgow: Drew, 1986)

Hudd, Roy, *Music Hall* (London: Methuen, 1976)

Irving, Gordon, *The Good Auld Days* (London: Jupiter Books, 1977)

Jay, Ricky, *Learned Pigs and Fireproof Women* (London: Hale, 1987)

Louvish, Simon, *Stan and Ollie* (London: Faber and Faber, 2001)

Mackenzie, Peter, *Reminiscences of Glasgow Vol. 1*, (Glasgow: John Tweed, 1865)

Maloney, Paul, *Scotland and the Music Hall, 1850–1914* (Manchester: Manchester University Press, 2003)

Mander, Raymond and Mitchenson, Joe, *British Music Hall* (Gentry Books, 1974)

Marshall, Michael, *Top Hat and Tails: The Story of Jack Buchanan* (London: Elm Tree Books, 1978)

McCabe, John, *The Comedy World of Stan Laurel* (London: Chrysalis Books Group, 2004)

M'Dowall, John K. *The People's History of Glasgow* (Wakefield: S. R. Publications, 1970)

Mellar, G.J., *The Northern Music Hall* (Newcastle: Graham, 1970)

Newton, Henry Chance, *Idols of the Halls* (London: 1928)

Rust, Brian, *British Music Hall on Record* (Harrow: General Gramophone Publications, 1979)

Wallace, William, *Harry Lauder in the Limelight*, (Lewes: Book Guild, 1988)

Woods, Roger and Lead, Brian, *Showmen or Charlatans? The Stories of 'Dr' Walford Bodie and 'Sir' Alexander Cannon* (Rossendale, Lancashire: 2005)

Wordsall, Frank, *A Glasgow Keek Show* (Glasgow: Richard Drew, 1981)

NEWSPAPERS AND JOURNALS

The Bailie

Barr's Professional Gazette

Daily Record

The Era

Evening Times

Glasgow Sentinel

Glasgow Herald

Glasgow Journal

Glasgow Mercury

Glasgow Sentinel

New York Telegraph

North British Daily Mail

The Programme

Records of the Burgh of Glasgow

The Showman

World's Fair

ILLUSTRATIONS CREDITS

The publisher would like to thank the following for their permission to reproduce images in the book. Every effort has been made to contact copyright holders, but it has not been possible to do so in every case. We would be please to receive any further information.

Note: Illustrations which appear in the colour section are indicated by (CS).

Gerald Barry: Florrie Bow Wow (CS)

Euan Adamson: pp. 9, 29, 36, 42, 62, 108, 162, 165, 166, 167; auditorium from arch, balcony entrance, exit sign, balcony from arch, ceiling arch, artefacts, Four Daisies poster, 1906 poster, rescue from a fire poster, 'Good acts wanted' poster, Tom Thumb poster

Minty Donald: p. 2; exterior of Britannia (CS)

Antony Duda: pp. 95, 116, 139

Glasgow University Library, Special Collections: pp. 18, 81

The Herald & Evening Times Picture Archive: pp. 127, 160

Graham Hunter: pp. 33, 40, 47, 57, 66, 78, 86, 88, 91, 94, 99, 102, 114, 119, 128, 130, 131, 132, 135, 137, 138, 150, 155; postcard of Laurel and Hardy (CS)

James Kelly / Britannia Panopticon Trust: p. 75

Mitchell Library: p. 15; Britannia programme (CS)

Peter Longman and the Theatres Trust: pp. 8, 23

Paul Maloney: p. 55

Teylers Museum Haarlem: Solomon poster (CS)

David Walker: p. 26; auditorium from balcony entrance (CS)

INDEX

Note: Page numbers in italics refer to illustrations.